Vireyas

Vireyas
A Practical Gardening Guide

Jacqueline Walker

& John Kenyon

Timber Press
Portland, Oregon

Acknowledgements: The authors are grateful to: Keith Adams, Os Blumhardt, Glyn Church, Michael Cullinane, Felix Jury, Mark and Abbie Jury, Bryan McDonald, Sue McLean, Liz Morrow, Brian and Jan Oldham, Graeme Rouse, Jim Rumble, Sylvia Saperstein, J. Clyde Smith, E. White Smith and Lucie Sorensen Smith, Graham Smith, Graham Snell, Jan Velvin and Rita Watson.

Photograph credits: Yvonne Cave, 14 (above left), 18, 21, 23 (right), 26, 28 (below), 29, 32, 38, 47, 49 (above), 50, 60 (left), 69 (2); Shelley Foster, 12, 49 (below); Gil Hanly, 8 (2), 14 (above right, below), 15, 16, 20, 22 (above), 24, 25, 31 (left) 33, 34, 36, 39, 40, 42, 43, 44, 45, 46, 51, 52 (2), 54, 57, 58, 60 (right), 63 (2), 64, 66, 67, 68, 70, 72 (below), 77; Jack Hobbs, 2, 10, 23 (left), 28 (above), 30, 48, 56, 71, 72 (above), 74; Anna Kilgour Wilson, 78; E. White Smith, 22 (below), 31 (right), 54, 58

First published in North America in 1997 by
Timber Press, Inc.
The Haseltine Building
133 S. W. Second Avenue, Suite 450
Portland, Oregon, 97204, USA
1-800-327-5680 (USA and Canada only)

© 1997 text: Jacqueline Walker and John Kenyon; photographs, as credited; this production: Godwit Publishing

ISBN 0 88192 402 4

A CIP record for this book is available from the Library of Congress.

Cover photograph: 'Tropic Glow' (Yvonne Cave).
Opposite title page: Hybrid *lochae* x *javanicum* (Jack Hobbs)
Typesetting and production: Kate Greenaway
Printed in Singapore

Contents

Foreword

A common misconception is that vireya rhododendrons are a comparatively recent introduction. In fact, they have been in cultivation for over 150 years.

This welcome new volume traces the history of their introduction from the time the Dutch colonised the East Indies, acknowledging the contribution made by the Dutch botanist Dr Hermann Sleumer in his manuscript *Flora Malesia*, and by seed collectors from New Zealand, America, Australia and the United Kingdom.

Collecting vireya species in the wild is not easy work, and there are still areas to be explored. We still have much to learn that will keep hobbyists, collectors and botanists busy for years to come.

In the meantime gardeners are reaping the benefits of hybridising. The old adage of 'hybrid vigour' applies particularly to vireyas. This book explains the relationship of species to hybrids and gives advice on selecting hybrids and their care and nurture, along with ideas for the ornamental use of vireyas. As more and more people come to know and grow these hybrids, they will value this handbook for its role in stimulating a new era in the cultivation and appreciation of vireya rhododendrons.

E. White Smith
Tacoma, Washington, USA
December 1996

Introduction

In any gardening lifetime there's a good chance that some special plant will capture and hold attention — first perhaps as a novelty — before becoming an acknowledged mainstay of the garden. It may be a genuinely new discovery — although major botanical discoveries are rare occurrences nowadays — or some clever hybridisation success, or a naturally occurring chance hybrid, or perhaps an already known plant plucked from obscurity. The vireya is all of these. Known and cultivated for over a century, but mostly within the confines of a few public collections and several more private ones, the vireya has previously never had wide horticultural exposure. Currently it is the subject of unprecedented attention with the promise of greater interest in future as its attributes become more widely known.

The vireya is a shrub for all seasons and all gardens. Evergreen, it is both an indoor-outdoor plant in cool climates with mild summers, and a fully outdoor plant for warmer climates with mild winters. Left unchecked, some vireyas will, over time, reach tree-like dimensions but in general they form small shrubs. The smallest varieties have leaves which are barely distinguishable from azalea leaves, the size of a newborn infant's finger. Larger vireyas have thick trunks and robust leaves the size of an adult's hand.

With their luminous flowers, often scented and always alluring, their repeat-flowering habit and their ease of culture (once understood), vireyas are gaining an ardent following. Their introduction into western gardens has stimulated the worldwide interest of horticulturalists, plant breeders, landscapers and other professionals — as well as home gardeners. And it is primarily for amateur growers that this book is written.

The text makes no claim to be authoritative. It has been a challenge to adapt the focus of the book to growers in diverse climates. The speculative aspect of introducing this relatively new shrub into domestic culture must be stressed; the authors have been motivated by their own enthusiasm and experience, and the often anecdotal contributions of other growers. At the same time, their twenty years of experience in growing vireyas (with increasing success over that period) amounts to a body of information and advice worth sharing. It should be noted, too, that among experienced growers there is little dissent concerning cultivation methods. Market growers, hybridists, collectors, nurserymen and hobbyists have contributed to a growing repository of practical expertise that is surprisingly consistent and which underscores the cultural advice given in a later chapter.

'Bob's Crowing Glory' (above) and 'Souvenir de J.H. Mangles'

A word about nomenclature. 'Vireya' is a common and popularly used name derived from a group, section Vireya, within the large genus *Rhododendron* to which these plants belong. The name was published in 1826 in honour of the French pharmacist and natural historian Julien Joseph Virey. Other names have been used. For some time vireyas were referred to as 'Malesian rhododendrons', Malesia being a botanically defined area in the tropics incorporating the Malay archipelago, New Guinea, the Philippines, Indonesia and neighbouring islands. If this botanical region is to include all vireyan habitats, then it extends to the east as far as Bougainville and the Solomon Islands; to the north as far as Taiwan; and to the south to include the northern part of Queensland in Australia.

One name which has gained wide popularity is 'tropical rhododendron', again a misleading term if considered descriptive of cultivation requirements. The natural habitat of many species is high in altitude, modifying the effect of the tropical latitude. The term 'subtropical rhododendron' may therefore be more apt, but since hybridising has taken the best and most useful qualities of vireyas from mixed altitudes to produce garden plants with as much temperature tolerance as possible, 'subtropical' may also be inappropriate. Other names include 'Hawaiian rhododendron' (botanically and geographically inaccurate), 'lepidote rhododendron' (botanically more accurate), and 'Java rhododendron'.

'Vireya' is the preferred name. It avoids confusion and is not geographically limiting or climatically descriptive. Another, if trifling, difficulty which the writing of this book posed for the authors has been how to refer to the other, non-vireyan rhododendrons. Repetitious use of 'Non-vireyan rhododendrons' was obviously tiresome. It seems best to refer to them simply as rhododendrons.

Perhaps the most exciting aspect of vireya culture is the landscaping and design possibilities it offers. In the introduction to her book *Garden Design*, British landscape architect Dame Sylvia Crowe speaks of some gardens as invoking 'immense peace, while others give a sense of exhilaration . . .'. Who has not known such feelings? For the beholder of the vireya garden there may be another kind of response: seduction. It's easy to be captivated.

What is a vireya?

A vireya is a rhododendron. It belongs to a clearly defined category within the genus *Rhododendron*, which in turn is part of the larger botanical family Ericaceae. The genus consists of some 900 species, more than 300 of which are vireyas.

As one third of the genus, it is no meagre portion. Yet the potential of vireyas as ornamentals has remained largely untapped until recent times. As new hybrids have been introduced and their cultural requirements and tolerances become better understood, there has been a steady increase in their popularity.

Although very variable, vireyas are nonetheless easily recognisable. The two features that distinguish them from other rhododendrons and azaleas are the scales that cover the leaves, stems and sometimes the flowers; and the long-tailed seeds.

The scales are discernible to the naked eye and are evident when touched; a thick coating can be dislodged when a leaf is held between thumb and forefinger. Under a microscope they're revealed as disc- or star-shaped; none are symmetrical, and although these identifying marks can reliably distinguish vireyas from others in the genus, botanists are unsure as to the scales' purpose.

Dr George Argent, in *Rhododendrons of Sabah*, considered the theory that scales may repel herbivores, and observed that because they are similar to bromeliad scales they may aid in the absorption and retention of water. He also suggested that the scales may shield new growth from solar radiation. As an example he gave the species *R. polyanthemum*, whose scale covering at maturity is sparse but whose young shoots are screened with a thick covering. Similarly, *R. crassifolium* has green mature leaves with 'hardly a scale to be found on the upper surface, yet the young unfolding leaves are . . . white with scales'; the scales turn brown and drop off as the leaf ages. Argent observed that, although the covering was light-reflecting when dry, the underlying colour of the leaf was clearly revealed when wet, allowing 'increased transmission of light to the inside of the leaf where the chlorophyll is situated.'

As for the other distinguishing feature of the vireya, magnification is not needed to see the long seed tails. Departing petals leave behind firm fruit pods, which ripen from the tips downwards. As the pods split open they reveal tiny seeds starting to darken in colour, with long, finely crimped tails at both ends. Two-tailed seeds are peculiar to vireyas; other rhododendrons have none or only one appendage. Botanists

Opposite: The handsome hybrid 'Lulu', with dark green leaves and flowers in four stages: bud, pale newly opened bloom, truss of fully opened flowers, and (left) stalk and seed pod left after petals have fallen.

'Lemon Lovely'

have reasoned that the tails give the wind-dispersed seeds extra buoyancy, enabling them to drift long distances, often over areas of dense vegetation. Because so much of their natural habitat may not be conducive to the establishment of seedlings, because the tropics are not known to be especially windy, and also because the seeds have a shorter period of viability than other rhododendrons, it follows that the better the seeds are able to float on air currents, the better their chances of reaching a suitable site and germinating within a short period of time. This form of dispersal is also advantageous for epiphytic plants, a habit adopted by many vireyas.

There are other, more variable characteristics that, although not botanically important, help distinguish vireyas from a horticultural perspective. Perhaps the most obvious, and certainly the most remarked upon, is vireyas' ability to flower more than once a year. This is, of course, the selling point used by commercial producers in the mass market. And why not? Why grow a shrub which brings pleasure once a year when its cousin will bring that pleasure twice or three times? Flowering times seem to be irregular, but for many growers, it's this uncertainty that appeals. Unlike other rhododendrons, which flower at approximately the same time every year — triggered by seasonal changes — vireyas may flower at different times in different years with almost mischievous unpredictability. The gardener who hovers and waits in vain for an untried vireya to bloom can tire of the exercise, banishing the potted plant from its place of prominence — only to rediscover it, a week later, aglow with smouldering embers. It's true that the flowering habit of some vireyas is in keeping with the rest of the genus, blooming once every year at about the same time. But it's also true that many species and even more hybrids flower twice a year; some hybrids flower three or four times a year. And it's true, too, that healthy plants of certain cultivars do in fact flower non-stop.

The explanation for this is that the plant has many budding stems, and different ones flower at different times. Close monitoring of a plant which flowers four times a year is likely to show a different part of the bush flowering each time, so that although the bush may appear to flower four times, in fact one quarter may flower in June, a second quarter in September, and so on. Still, some growers will challenge this and claim that the same stems produce buds over and over throughout the year. Perhaps they do. However the flowering is perceived, no one would disagree that the vireya's ability to bloom continuously is its trump card.

Whereas other types of rhododendrons are attuned to a strong seasonal rhythm, vireyas appear to be less affected by season. Day and night lengths in their natural habitat are almost unvaried, so in cultivation, flowering may be as much influenced by changes in moisture supply as any other factor, but this remains a subject of debate.

It seems to be an intriguing peculiarity of the vireya that it can produce a steadily growing bud which swells to the brink of opening, only to suspend its development. Weeks or even months later, it will suddenly burst forth. While this is going on, another vireya will go from being bare of bud to full-budded and thence to flowering — all in a flash. Indeed, bud behaviour excels at deception.

So it's difficult to draw firm conclusions about flowering patterns, and probably all that can be agreed upon is that flowering varies greatly. But there is another difference: as vireya flowers age their colour deepens; the flowers of other rhododendrons fade. More time and more monitoring of vireya flowering may yield clearer patterns.

Flower colours range from pure white through cream, yellow, orange, salmon, pink, to deep red and almost maroon, and enthusiasts can become quite lyrical in describing these colours. Azalea and non-vireya rhododendron growers, especially show exhibitors, may disagree with the opinion — and opinion it is — that vireyas come in colours of greater clarity, depth and intensity than other rhododendrons, or indeed than most other garden flowers. Perhaps these intense colours help lure pollinators. Names like 'Hot Tropic', 'Fireball', 'Fire Halo', 'Tropic Glow' and 'Fire Flash' are apt. Some colours are simply dazzling. Perhaps these electric hues can be linked to the vireya's habitat high on the slopes of rugged equatorial mountains, where the periods of swirling mist and dense cloud alternate with brilliantly clear skies and high ultraviolet levels.

Perhaps this is why in South Pacific countries where the light is equally bright — bright enough for jet-lagged travellers from northern winters to exclaim at the clarity of the air and the searing sun — the vireya seems so at home. And perhaps, like the hibiscus of Hawaii, which gained popularity elsewhere before becoming the symbol of its homeland, the vireya may one day become symbolic of gardens in the southern subtropics.

Another characteristic which can be said to describe the vireya, and with more scientific rigour than such discussions of colour, is flower form. Flower trusses are often more sparse or lank than the full trusses of other rhododendrons. This may change with further breeding, since the latter have had the advantage of many more years of breeding to produce the showy, often ruffle-petalled, densely packed trusses seen today. But the individual flowers which make up the vireya's truss are usually more loosely arranged and often elongated at the base, as evident in the predominance of tubular and salver forms. Species such as *R. herzogii*, *R. longiflorum*, *R. loranthiflorum*, *R. tuba*, *R. jasminiflorum*, *R. praetervisum* and *R. suaveolens* have notably long and narrow

The pendulous bell flowers of the hybrid 'St Valentine'

R. tuba, a species with conspicuously long tubular flowers, pleasantly scented

'Just Peachy', a very floriferous hybrid

R. stenophyllum, in flower and leaf unlike almost all
other vireyas

corolla tubes, often as long as 12 cm. This is a conspicuous vireyan trait. There are usually five petals, although some, such as the large and lavish flowers of *R. leucogigas*, have more.

Then there are the leaves, which even a casual observer can soon identify as vireyan. Some surprises exist, though, to confuse even the experienced eye. In general, the leaves are produced in whorls with each new shoot appearing from the centre of the whorl. The mature leaves are strong, often thick, not easily torn, shiny on the upper surface, and so designed that water passes quickly off.

From the largest to the smallest, from the narrowest to the broadest, the leaf variation encompasses a range as wide as that of other groups within the genus. The leaves of *R. konori* are among the largest, up to 30 cm long and 10 cm wide in cultivation. Those of *R. gracilentum* are among the smallest, 10 mm long and 3 mm wide. The circular leaves of *R. blackii* are the extreme opposite of the astonishingly narrow leaves of *R. stenophyllum*. Probably the most perplexing leaf of all vireyas is that of *R. ericoides*, an alpine species that is aptly named as it all but succeeds in passing itself off as an alpine heather and is quite unlike any other vireya.

Bush shape varies too. In the wild it is common for vireyas to be rangy and straggly, rarely compact — alpine species are the exception — and always growing in competition with other plants. Under cultivation their different growth habits are more apparent. Some are upright, some compact, others spreading and even prostrate.

With some exceptions mature leaves have their upper sides on view as open, usually glossy surfaces with visible veins. In healthy bushes such foliage makes for marvellous garden shrubs even without flowers. Some are highly coloured. The leaves of the cultivar 'Hugh Redgrove', for example, are a rich bronze-red. Vireya leaves are rarely eaten by bugs, which prefer to chew on more tender foliage. Both leaves and flowers, incidentally, are poisonous to humans and animals.

15

A sampling of the wide variety of vireya leaves

In their native habitats they frequently grow as epiphytes, in some cases growing only epiphytically. Speculation that this serves to further distinguish vireyas from others in the genus is common. Certainly it's a characteristic much in evidence. Examples of both above-ground and on-ground specimens of the same species have led to the conclusion that vireyas in general appear to grow epiphytically more often and more readily than other rhododendrons. Although botanically this does not distinguish the group, it is certainly a guide for their cultivation in the home garden, making them ideally suited to container culture. Root confinement never bothers them.

Species are plants that occur naturally with particular genetic characteristics that occur naturally. They are reproductively isolated so that they retain their distinct identity. Hybrids, on the other hand, are the plants that result from the crossing of two separate and distinct individuals. Nomenclature sets out three conditions for plants to be considered species: they must differ from their closest relations in at least two characteristics; they must differ in geographic distribution; and they must differ in ecological distribution, i.e. in their growth requirements. Natural interspecific hybrids often occur in the wild. In horticulture, intentional hybridising is aimed at producing plants with the best and most desirable qualities of both parents. Vireya hybridising includes the cross of species with species, of species with hybrids, and back-crossing.

Purists invariably prefer species to hybrids. In the words of Graham Smith, Director of Pukeiti Rhododendron Park in New Zealand, 'Species are perceived by the purists to be pure, unadulterated and rather classy, which tends to give them an exclusive appeal.' Their diversity fascinates. Botanists and collectors enjoy the challenge of growing only species for, as with many other garden plants, the species are more difficult to grow; hybrids are generally easier. There are exceptions, of course, but for the beginner the easiest, most reliable vireya hybrids are recommended — the more so since most gardeners seek flowers, and hybrids flower more than species.

16

Vireyas in cultivation

Past and present

The history of the vireya's introduction to the western world, and of the first hybridising programme, starts with the Veitch Nursery in England. John Veitch, the nursery's founder, originally trained in an Edinburgh nursery in the mid-eighteenth century before being appointed estate steward to Sir Thomas Acland in Exeter. Such was Veitch's skill that his employer became his patron, setting him up with a nursery of his own on land with a lifetime lease. By the time of John Veitch's death, his son James had taken over the nursery, now relocated to freehold land, and under his direction the business thrived. Veitch plant collectors went all over the world. Their names — and the names of their patrons, and of the hybridisers who worked with the new species they obtained — have been perpetuated in the naming of species: *R. lobbii* (named after collector Thomas Lobb, but now known as *R. longiflorum*), *R. taylorii* (after George Taylor, a hybridiser), and *R. curtisii* (after collector Charles Curtis), among others.

The nursery expanded and by 1853 had moved to Kings Road in Chelsea, where it became famous for its exotic introductions, using heated glasshouses to provide tropical or semi-tropical conditions. They bred a mind-boggling 500 or more vireya hybrids from a mere handful of original species: *R. jasminiflorum, R. javanicum, R. l. ookeanum, R. longiflorum, R. malayanum, R. multicolor* and *R. teysmannii* (now known to be a form of *R. javanicum*).

Dedicated, intensive work went on. What became of all 500 hybrids is largely unknown, even allowing for those which would have been considered unworthy of further propagation. Of the worthy ones, only six have survived the ensuing century. These, still commonly grown today, are: 'Princess Alexandra', 'Pink Seedling', 'Clorinda', 'Princess Royal', 'Ne Plus Ultra' and 'Souvenir de J. H. Mangles'. The nursery even produced a group of semi-double to double-flowered forms, which were named 'balsamaeflorum' after the double flowers of some balsams.

The hybrid with the long name, 'Souvenir de J. H. Mangles', was named in honour of a prominent gardening writer and plantsperson of the time, who after visiting the Veitch nursery for the first time in 1879 described: 'dark green and glossy foliage, and on one . . . several trusses of expanded flowers such as I have never seen before. The colour was a peculiarly striking crimson, the truss many-flowered, and each well poised member of the umbel showed itself to perfection.'

Opposite: An unnamed hybrid seedling

This response typifies the impact that these lusciously exotic and vibrant flowering shrubs had upon Europeans at that time. Such was the level of interest that there must surely have been other nurseries and other hybridists in Britain and elsewhere who took up the breeding challenge, but little is known of them. A few were eventually imported to New Zealand, because an early catalogue from an Otago nursery included two species. But it was the Veitch creations that became the celebrated showpieces of many a Royal Horticultural Society meeting in England, where they maintained their sensational and exclusive status — exclusive because only those gardeners and estate owners wealthy enough to own heated glasshouses could grow them — up until the end of the nineteenth century.

Then vireyas disappeared from sight. The First World War, the Depression and the Second World War all took their toll. The luxury of fuel-heated glasshouses could not be sustained for something as indulgent as growing ornamental plants other than by botanic gardens and a few large estates. And because by the early part of this century collectors from China and the Himalayas had introduced hardy rhododendrons which would grow year-round outside, the tender type soon gave way to the hardy.

It wasn't until the middle of this century that interest in vireyas was rekindled. The opening up of New Guinea by missionaries, miners and gold prospectors increased interest in the country's botanical riches. One botanist in particular, Dr Hermann Sleumer, who in the early 1960s mapped out vireyas from the Malay Peninsula to New Guinea, can be credited with lighting the way. Sleumer described a plethora of new species in the 1960s and through his collections many species became available

R. goodenoughii, a species with white, scented flowers

R. jasminiflorum, a species with long tubular flowers in ice pink, fragrant.

for general cultivation. The full impact of the importance of the section Vireya came when it was realised that it comprised one third of the genus Rhododendron.

In New Zealand, one of the earliest collections was housed in the famous rhododendron park at Pukeiti on the northern slopes of Mt Taranaki. The first cuttings and seedlings came from Ewen Perrott, Keith Adams and Felix Jury among others, and by 1976 a collection of 100 plants was thriving in a specially constructed display house. The collection was considerably augmented in the late 1970s and 1980s by contributions from Australian and New Zealand collectors. Director Graham Smith brought back material from Papua New Guinea and the collection continues to grow today. Pukeiti now has more than 100 species and as many hybrids. Other notable collections open to the public include the Australian Rhododendron Society's garden at Mt Pleasant, near Wollongong in New South Wales, and the Strybing Arboretum in San Francisco (see appendix).

Meanwhile, hybridisers were at work. New Zealand hybridists who have registered cultivars include: Ewen Perrott; Graham Smith; Os Blumhardt, responsible for the introduction of many other quality plants besides vireyas; Michael Cullinane, who gave particular attention to high-altitude miniatures; Felix Jury, who introduced the species *R. macgregoriae* to New Zealand and used it to create a number of very successful hybrids, and later his son Mark; and hybridists working at the Duncan and Davies nursery in New Plymouth, who have been responsible for some highly regarded releases.

Australian breeders have dramatically increased the number of impressive hybrids. The work done by John Rouse, Graham Snell, Bob Withers, Tom Lelliot, Don Stanton and Sylvia Sapperstein among others is documented in Australian records, while in

21

An early hybrid 'Ne Plus Ultra'

A recently bred hybrid 'Red Adair'

'Golden Charm'   'Rangitoto Rose'

the United States important hybridising has been done by John Evans, Jock Brydon and Peter Sullivan at Stribing Arboretum, and by Arnie Jenson, Frank Mossman and Bill Moynier.

All hybridising is done purposefully, the donor parents being selected for their desirable properties. The criteria used to decide which offspring from a particular cross is worthy of commercial propagation include the following: good form with a bushy growth habit; attractive foliage; good strong trusses and fullness of truss; flower size; flower colour; cold- or heat-tolerance, ideally both; flowering qualities; ability to repeat flower; and scent.

An observation made recently by a New Zealand horticultural writer was that hybridists appeared to be moving in different directions. He observed that while one hybridist looked for a bushy habit and good leaf quality besides flowers, another sought miniature flowers and form, while a third concentrated on showy flowers above all else, even double-flowered forms aimed at appealing to the 'rosebud market'.

In Australia, where vireyas are now established as the shrub to brighten the warm subtropical areas of New South Wales and Queensland, the demand has been for large, lavish and voluptuous blooms — the bigger the better — in strong and dazzling colours.

The future

It is now generally believed there are still species awaiting discovery, particularly in New Guinea. It is also possible that some plants originally described as species may prove to be natural hybrids. Some enthusiasts cling to the hope that somewhere in the world other forgotten early hybrids from the nineteenth century are still in existence and may be saved from the brink of obscurity.

With different hybridists taking different tacks, gardeners in the future will have an increasing number of hybrids to tempt them in an ever-expanding range and will be able to select cultivars bred for specific situations and which appeal to different tastes. It is likely there will be so many high-quality hybrids that some of the lesser performers grown today will be eliminated. Some rigorous culling will strengthen the cause.

At present there are about 400 named hybrids and many unamed ones: not bad for a couple of decades' work. Yet in terms of potential, they're but a trickle from a brimming genetic reservoir, a reservoir that in the next century will produce an outpouring.

One trait with obvious potential that will undoubtedly bolster future markets is greater cold-tolerance of higher-altitude vireyas. More of these smaller-leaved species are becoming available all the time. Dwarf hybrids are part of this thrust to meet the requirements of a geographically expanding market, and in North America in particular (for obvious climatic reasons) much attention has been given to these 'cooler climate' types.

There's potential to extend the colour spectrum beyond the present range. New colours may push the limits from deep pink into maroons and magentas. There may be developments in lemon and lime-green colours. And in time vireya flowers with contrasting etching on the petal margins, banding or textured petals may become available.

Also awaiting wider recognition is the vireya's potential in floral art. The day has yet to come when receivers of gift baskets and bouquets wax rhapsodic over vireya

'Maid Marion'

Vireyas have great potential for use in floral art

blooms. In the cut-flower market the vireya may never outflank the rose, but it will surely make a stand. The few florists who have used them have confined their arrangements to tight bunches of blooms rather than long-stemmed cuttings as structural components

There's much trial work to be done in this regard, such as determining the best picking time, which appears to be at bud opening, and establishing which vireyas are most suitable as cut flowers. On average, the vase life is about 5–10 days, which, by the standards of the industry, is not long. However, there are many reports of flowers lasting longer and it is clear that pollination drastically shortens flower longevity. An Australian grower of 'Highland Arabesque', the stamens of which produced sterile pollen so that there was no self-fertilisation, reported blooms that lasted twelve days. Graham Smith of Pukeiti reported that, 'Two flowers on *helwigii* had their stamens removed as soon as they opened for pollen collecting. These flowers then lasted nearly three weeks on the bush. It was obvious that 'selfing' the first truss caused the corollas to drop prematurely. I wonder if this has been observed in other vireyas, as indeed it is a well known fact with orchids.'

There's also the vireya's foliage. Once florists see the possibilities of using the leaves of cultivars such as 'Cyprian', creative ideas will flow. Decorative opportunities are everywhere; for example wedding bouquets of perhaps 'Pink Ray', *R. jasminiflorum*, *R. loranthiflorum*, and 'Felicitas' may soon be regularly gracing bridal settings. As one florist expressed it: 'We are thoroughly tired of carnations and chrysanthemums and would welcome something new.' They shall have it.

Vireyas in the wild

Over the past thirty years or more many plant hunters, both trained botanists and amateurs, have visited Southeast Asia, western Malaysia and New Guinea in search of vireyas. They've roughed it out in rugged terrain, plunged through insect-ridden swamps, and ascended high, exposed ridges to altitudes of 4,500 metres. They've gone to record and classify, to bring back seeds for germination and cuttings for propagation (having first obtained the necessary permits), while some have gone just to look.

Descriptions of what they saw are helpful to gardeners growing vireyas in domestic settings. These accounts can enable amateurs to grow vireyas not just as well as in their natural habitats — for in the wild this means broken, torn or chewed plants — but to grow them better. This collection of field observations serves as a preamble to the following chapter on cultivation.

Felix Jury, a renowned plant hybridist from Taranaki in New Zealand, went to Papua New Guinea on a plant-hunting expedition in 1958. Among the species he saw were *R. phaeochitum*, *R. quadrasianum*, and *R. womersleyi*. He collected cuttings of *R. macgregoriae* and *R. leptanthum*, the original plants of which still thrive in his Urenui garden. He saw these vireyas as colonisers, growing not on forest floors or in crowded valleys, but in clearings, appearing always in the wake of the axe: 'As the local inhabitants made cuttings in the forest with their stone axes to plant their corn and kumara [apparently all they lived on], the colonising plants would follow. The vireya is to the New Guinea highlands what the tree fern and manuka are to New Zealand.' The soil he described as 'astonishingly heavy clay, so heavy that even on steep slopes at 7,000 feet where missionaries had dug one-metre deep holes for planting coffee, the water didn't drain away.' That is why the vireyas 'were growing *on* the ground, not in it.' In a place where 200 inches or more of rain falls annually, and where even the dry season means a daily shower of rain 'bucketing down', vireyas obviously obtain sufficient moisture to meet their needs in positions on top of the ground or, as Felix Jury was not alone in observing, growing on other plants. Vireyas have been recorded growing in tree forks as high as 30 metres above ground.

Two botanists from the Leyden National Herbarium in Holland made an extensive expedition to New Guinea to study ericaceous plants in 1961. Dr Hermann Sleumer and Dr Pieter van Royen reported their findings in botanical journals, and extracts

Opposite: Hybrid 'Dr Hermann Sleumer' x *leucogigas*

The species *R. macgregoriae*, seen here in full flush, is an early introduction from New Guinea.

Two hybrids with *R. macgregoriae* as a parent: 'Rob's Favourite' (left) and 'Yellow Ball'

from van Royen's descriptions of habitats and climatic and soil conditions are reproduced here, while Sleumer's classification has become internationally recognised. Sleumer's pioneering work resulted in the naming and identification of many hitherto unknown species, later published in *An Account of Rhododendron in Malesia Flora* and *Rhododendrons in New Guinea*.

Sleumer discovered and named *R. leucogigas*, a deserving name (meaning 'white giant') for so robust a plant with huge leaves and large scented flowers. At Ormu, at sea level on the northern coast of Papua New Guinea, he recorded *R. zoelleri* growing epiphytically on trees, a species he had previously seen flourishing epiphytically at altitudes of 1800 metres and higher. He later found it at Tanahmerah Bay, again at sea level, this time growing as a tree with 'a straight trunk over eight metres high'. Such wide-ranging examples surprised him. He was able to establish that this species grew in a wider range of altitudes and conditions than probably any other. Unsurprisingly, *R. zoelleri* has been used to produce more hybrids than almost any other. The implication for the home gardener is that hybrids involving this species can be expected to be very adaptable.

Sleumer observed that vireyas occurred wherever the earth had been disturbed or the trees removed by landslides. 'The production of seeds in large quantities and their distribution by wind makes possible such initial settlements. The same thing occurs when the natives burn down the trees.' He reasoned that both epiphytes in the crowns of trees and terrestrial plants in clearings would receive the same amount of light. In one of the most unlikely of habitats, he found *R. aurigeranum* growing on the edge of a forest 'more or less encircled by dry grassland where it had survived frequent grass fires'. This, though, was exceptional.

Sleumer's colleague, Dr Pieter van Royen, kept records of climates and temperatures

'Dr Hermann Sleumer', named after the pioneering botanist

R. aurigeranum x *R. macgregoriae*

conducive to vireya growth. In his 'Field Observations on Rhododendron in New Guinea', published in the *American Rhododendron Society Journal* in April 1984, van Royen wrote that after 22 years of observing the conditions under which vireyas grow in New Guinea, he'd reached the conclusion that although a few species flourished within only a very narrow temperature range, for most species the conditions were varied and variable. He wrote: 'The main temperature belt where most species are found is that between 60 and 70°F at altitudes of 3000–4500 ft, and between 55 and 65°F at altitudes of 9000–10,000 ft. In the lower levels the lowest temperatures do not appear important, but at the 10,000 ft level night temperatures drop to about 40°F. In this belt we find such species as *R. aurigeranum*, *R. dianthosmum*, *R. helwigii*, *R. herzogii*, *R. laetum* and *R. superbum*. In the alpine regions where the average day temperature ranges from 33–40°F, and almost every night drops below freezing, we find *R. rubellum* and *R. saxifragoides*. Both are found as low as 10,000 ft, but reach their best . . . between 10,000 and 14,000 ft. Both species are found where the sun bakes the grasslands from May to September, while for the rest of the year heavy rain, mists, hail and snow dominate the grasslands.'

Humidity also seemed variable. Alpine regions have a lower humidity than thickly forested valleys and lowlands, so he assumed alpine species such as *R. commonae* and *R. saxifragoides* to be tolerant of lower humidity. He observed that the presence of thicker leaves indicated an ability to grow under drier conditions than plants with thinner leaves, which were found in more humid areas.

Light, he found, seemed to play a more important part than humidity. Ultraviolet light increases with altitude. Van Royen observed that flower trusses tended to be larger and fuller in sun than in shade, and that the higher-altitude species in New Guinea tended to have red flowers whereas those of low-altitude species were more likely to be white, yellow or orange. He thus speculated that the combined effects of decreased humidity and increased ultraviolet light resulted in plants with smaller, thicker leaves, fuller flower trusses and flowers of a deeper red than species growing 'in the shade of the subalpine shrubberies'. *R. commonae*, in particular, bore out this theory.

He also examined soil preferences. Although he found places of extreme acidity, the greater number of vireyas grew in soils with a pH reading of around 6–7.5. Some seemed to tolerate more alkaline soils, such as those near the limestone cliffs of eastern New Guinea, but he interpreted the more numerous vireyas in western Papua New Guinea as an indication of their preference for more acid soils.

Epiphytes grow in soils composed of decaying vegetable matter, particularly when found very high up in trees where, obviously, there is no ground soil. He saw soil which was 'usually highly porous and both dries out quickly and soaks up water quickly. The soil is often black or dark brown, and the root systems of the shrubs growing in it are small but well-developed. As a growth medium it is an extreme one. In nature epiphytic rhododendrons are small shrubs, poorly branched . . . the situation is somewhat different for epiphytes that grow lower down on the trunks. Often these species grow in moss cushions which maintain higher moisture levels. Their root systems are better developed.'

Terrestrial plants, on the other hand, grew in a variety of different New Guinea topsoils, which he found overlaid a loamy or clay subsoil which was at times very wet. He recorded some pH readings as low as 4.5 for soil supporting specimens of *R. rubellum* and *R. saxifragoides*. In many instances his soil samples were high in organic

R. helwigii, among the strongest-coloured reds

'Lucie Sorensen'

31

matter, the result of the continuous accumulation and breakdown of the surrounding vegetation. The topsoils were always found to be highly porous.

In 1965 and 1968, British veterinary surgeon Michael Black made several vireya-collecting trips to Papua New Guinea. His findings were published in an article 'Expedition to Malesia' in the Royal Horticultural Society's *Rhododendron and Camellia Year Book* 1970. He discovered a vireya peculiarity: while the root balls of most vireyas are small and often confined to pockets in tree crotches or logs and stumps, mature vireyas in certain circumstances possessed extensive root systems.

On an excursion to the upper reaches of the Fatima River he found: 'Many rhododendrons grew in the gravel and among the rocks on the banks, and in one place where the river had changed its course there were quite a number colonising the old river bed, which appeared to be pure sand and gravel.'

Black noted that vireyas frequently rooted in sphagnum moss. In drier areas he saw them growing in near-xerophytic conditions, observing that only mature plants seemed able to grow this way, as has been borne out by plants in cultivation. Young plants cannot survive without frequent watering.

Os Blumhardt, a plant breeder in Northland, New Zealand, has been cultivating vireyas since the 1950s. He made his first trip to Sabah in North Borneo in 1979, when he climbed to the top of Mt Kinabalu collecting *R. bagobonum* (which takes its name from the Bagobon tribe in the Philippines, where it also grows), *R. rugosum, R. stenophyllum, R. fallacinum, R. retivenium, R. polyanthemum* and *R. crassifolium*.

He made a second trip the following year with his brother. On this trip he found *R. suaveolens, R. praetervisum, R. crassifolium* and the species he was particularly seeking, *R. brookeanum*: 'All these species are normally epiphytes, and we saw plants . . . stuck on the bare trunks of trees with just a ring of roots around the trunk to hang on by.

'Tropic Glow' x *R. lochae*

R. javanicum

The best way to find epiphytes is to find fallen trees. We also found plants of *R. crassifolium*, *R. suaveolens* and one of *R. praetervisum* growing on roadside banks and these were the best we saw of their species.'

On a third trip in 1986, this time to New Guinea, Blumhardt collected pollen by storing it in folds of paper in an airtight package containing silica gel, and from that pollen he produced a number of very successful hybrids.

Graham Smith, Horticultural Director of Pukeiti Rhododendron Park in Taranaki, New Zealand, made two trips to New Guinea in 1983 and 1986, and one to the Cameroon Highlands in Malaysia. On each trip he was struck with the way vireyas blended into the local landscape. At first he couldn't even see them, especially if they were not in flower; after a while his 'eyes adjusted'. The plants' colonising habit was immediately apparent. They grew in clearings, and 'once the rest of the forest took over, they got sqeezed out. So unless they made it to a huge height, the vireyas would disappear', only to reappear in some other clearing.

In New Guinea he saw *R. superbum*, the scented, white-flowered species large of limb and truss, growing high in tree tops. Under cultivation *R. superbum* tends to be leggy and sparsely foliaged, yet here in the wild he saw it had a full, dense form. One of the largest vireyas he saw was a specimen of *R. macgregoriae* over 4 metres tall with a trunk diameter of 20 cm. Interestingly, he observed that many of these epiphytic species were also capable of growing terrestrially, while quite a few terrestrial species grew epiphytically, and 'some seemed to be neither one nor the other'.

As others before him had found, 'the higher you go, the more marginal vireyas become. And always they're along the edges of the forest. . . As a general rule, species become smaller and smaller in leaf with increasing altitude. *R. gracilentum* is probably the exception. '*R. macgregoriae* was the most common and widely distributed of all

33

R. konori

vireyas he saw, although at higher altitude *R. saxifragoides* was much in evidence. One *R. saxifragoides* he noticed 'had a taproot down through glacial rubble; it was growing in a hollow and the taproot must have been two and a half feet long'. Such taproots are exceptional.

His most surprising discovery was at Mt Gilawee, at an altitude of 2,800 metres: 'We were camped under canvas on the open grass beside the bush, and overnight there was a frost that left a covering of thick white ice. Vireyas which would have been unable to tolerate living in either the bush or the open grass were happily growing along the edge, clearly defined by the frost-free drip line of the trees.' Only in that narrow drip-line of protection, where they had neither frost to harm them nor the dense bush vegetation to shade them out, could they survive. Temperatures were below freezing; the frost was near them but not on them. Graham Smith believes that the dominant high-altitude species, *R. saxifragoides*, has hybridising potential for cold-tolerance, along with *R. retusum*, which grows at cooler altitudes in Sumatra.

In 1988, George Argent of the Edinburgh Botanic Gardens in Scotland, together with Anthony Lamb, Anthe Phillipps and Sheila Collenette, published the results of their field work in North Borneo. Their book *Rhododendrons of Sabah* identifies and describes 35 species and 7 natural hybrids. They established that 12 species exist only in Sabah, and that on Mt Kinabalu alone ('a rich hunting ground') there are 25 different species.

Argent established that the Ericaceae, the plant family to which all rhododendrons belong, is specially equipped with endotrophic mycorrhizae, 'an association between

34

their roots and a fungus, which appears to give them a tremendous advantage in obtaining nutrients under these acid conditions.'

To end this collection of encounters with vireyas in the wild are comments from John Kenyon, a vireya specialist in Tauranga, New Zealand, who visited Mt Kinabalu in 1995: 'Near headquarters I saw *R. crassifolium* in bud in moist, part-shade; another growing 40 ft up in a tree. *R. suaveolens* was growing in full sun. Other plants growing together with vireyas included orchids, ferns, mosses, palms, gingers, medinillas, tibouchinas, begonias, dracaenas, alocasias and scheffleras.'

The importance of microclimate became apparent when he saw, at 4,000 metres, the vireyas he expected to see, the mostly alpine types such as the tiny-leaved *R. ericoides* and *R. buxifolium*. But unexpectedly among them was the large-leaved *R. lowii*. Yet in each instance *R. lowii* had found its own pocket, its own special microclimate where it enjoyed more sheltered conditions. Elsewhere he saw *R. rugosum* growing in quite heavy shade displaying very long internodes on their stems, but the same species growing out of the shade had much shorter internodes. As with vireyas in cultivation, increased light produces a more compact and bushier habit.

Clearly, the conditions in which vireyas grow in their natural habitat are very diverse. It's also clear, though, that they have certain requirements which must be met if they are to thrive — or to grow at all — and that the most important of these is drainage. Where they inhabit bogs they grow on the margin of waterlogged ground, or above it, but never in it. They can even, as Michael Black saw, grow epiphytically on host plants that in turn are growing epiphytically on others.

Of those plants which grow high up in trees, it might be asked: how can large plants grow where seemingly they would have few nutrients? The frequent showers may perhaps also bear nitrogen from lightning, which is a common occurrence, and they may also bear dust and minerals from the fires of the natives living there; there would also be the decomposing bryophytes on which the seed germinated along with other organic litter.

If the most important requirement is drainage, the next important must be moisture. High rainfall is the norm. Showers are frequent and heavy, but quick to pass. Periods of drought do occur, causing minimal harm to mature plants. Another need is for air circulation. Although not described above, air circulation is an important part of their environment and it's easy to imagine how plants living high up would have no lack of air movement.

Imagining the setting and recreating such conditions can help in ensuring the optimal health and performance of vireyas grown in the garden.

KAY STROUD

Growing vireyas

Cultivation requirements

A well-grown vireya commands attention. Conversely, a poor specimen is quickly dismissed. When a 'new' garden shrub is neither widely grown nor its needs sufficiently understood, bare-branched stragglers can unfortunately set an example. Yet once you know how to grow them well, whole vistas of imagined plantings open up so that, aside from constraints of space or budget, the possibilities are unlimited.

Successful growers generally agree on the vireya's requirements, and the following advice is compiled from such sources. There are small differences of opinion. Fertilising practices vary and light levels are the subject of discussion. There are many recipes for potting mixes. In short, there is no single 'right' way to grow vireyas. To experiment is to learn.

Nonetheless, it is possible to identify the needs of vireyas. Their main requirements are:

- Shallow planting
- Excellent drainage
- Good light but protection from burning sun
- Protection from frost
- Regular light watering, although mature plants are more drought-tolerant
- Regular light feeding
- Mulching
- Undisturbed roots
- Good air circulation

It may be useful to note that among gardeners growing these plants for the first time, those who grow orchids successfully also usually grow vireyas well. This is because orchids have epiphytic preferences similar to vireyas in the wild residing in small niches where moisture and rain, though plentiful, drain rapidly away; they therefore have similar requirements in cultivation.

In general, and especially where plant performance is disappointing, it is helpful to bear in mind the vireya's natural habitat, as described in the previous chapter, and to provide similar conditions.

Opposite: 'Dawn Chorus'

Sunlight

There's considerable debate about the amount of direct sunlight vireyas will tolerate or need to thrive. When vireyas were still rather novel, gardeners were told to plant them in the hottest, most sun-soaked place they could find. It's now generally agreed that such advice is misleading Vireyas don't need all-day sun and are better off with some shade.

However, it's not as simple as this. Sun- and shade-tolerance seem to vary from species to species and from hybrid to hybrid. Sun for half the day seems to suit them well, although many will tolerate all-day sun. Morning sun is preferable to afternoon sun, which can result in quite stressful temperature and humidity levels in the late afternoon.

While some will tolerate almost full shade, more shade usually means less flowering. Some hybrids are slower to flower when grown in the shade. On the other hand, and somewhat frustratingly, the flowers that result from a sunny position may suffer from sunburn. In a situation where flowers are produced more profusely in a sunny site but look better in the shade, the choice is up to the grower. 'Brightly' is an example: in the shade its red-orange flowers really glow but plants flower best in sunnier positions. Vireyas that are shade-tolerant while still flowering well include 'Sweet Wendy', 'Popcorn', 'Pretty Cotton Candy', 'Rob's Favourite', 'Carillon Bells' and 'Fire Plum'.

Leaf colour may change according to exposure to sun, with greater exposure bringing out red and purple pigments. Leaf scorching can result from rapid changes in the amount of sun exposure.

'Sweet Wendy'

'Brightly'

Heat

Although vireyas hail from the tropics, they occur over a range of altitudes, with some species growing naturally at sea level, some high up in snow-dusted mountains, and many mid-way between the two. The name 'tropical rhododendrons' is especially misleading (as misleading, perhaps, as an advertisement appearing in the American Rhododendron Society's 1994 journal, which read 'Prepare for global warming: buy vireyas!'). Experience has shown that the many vireyas now in cultivation do better in temperate and subtropical climates rather than the tropics, and that probably the temperate end of the subtropical spectrum is ideal. In general, gardens with warm rather than hot summers, and mild winters, provide the most suitable conditions.

Bear in mind that heat tolerance is not necessarily the same as tolerance of full sun. Many hardened, acclimatised plants will tolerate full sun while remaining intolerant of excessive heat. A rough guide to temperature suitability is provided by leaf size and leaf surface texture. Most small-leaved vireyas dislike hot conditions, preferring cooler temperatures similar to the high-altitude, subalpine to alpine regions in tropical countries where they originate. Large leaves — and this is a generalisation — can indicate greater heat-tolerance, with the very large-leaved species and hybrids being the most heat-tolerant of all. Leaf surface may be a better guide: smooth, shiny leaves are indicative of heat-tolerance. So if you live at sea level in the subtropics, or have a particularly warm situation in your garden, seek out vireyas with large, smooth, shiny leaves.

The hybrid progeny of species originating in tropical latitudes at low altitude are the ones to select if you live in a very warm climate. Such species include *R. longiflorum*, *R. javanicum* (especially *R. javanicum* subsp. *brookeanum*), *R. christianae*, *R. loranthiflorum*, and *R. zoelleri*.

39

Cold

Vireyas cannot tolerate temperatures below freezing. See Frost damage, page 58, and Growing vireyas indoors, page 59.

Wind and air circulation

Vireyas like good air circulation. However, newly planted specimens can be blown over by the wind so staking may be necessary. In the wild, vireyas often start off their lives under parent plants where they receive sufficient shelter. If you garden on a really exposed site that is frequently lashed by howling gales, the best choice of vireyas are the lower-growing bushes, well staked and preferably sited between taller windbreaks. Your vireyas' foliage may suffer somewhat, but rarely from bugs or diseases.

Feeding, watering and mulching

FEEDING. Individual growers have had success with different methods of feeding, some using a slow-release fertiliser and others a faster-acting fertiliser in granular form. Others maintain that blood and bone in conjunction with well-made compost promotes plant health. The practice among most professionals today is a low-application feeding programme which is high in calcium, nitrogen and magnesium but low in potash potassium and phosphorus.

Like others in the genus, vireyas are intolerant of high potash levels, but unlike other rhododendrons and azaleas, they're intolerant of acid plant food; poultry manure is too alkaline and a commercial orchid fertiliser mix has been known to kill them. Although it can be said with certainty that vireyas prefer more acidic than alkaline media, it is not possible to dicate pH levels; they have proved capable of growing in a wide variety of conditions.

Several fertilisers are recommended. Brand names include Osmocote Plus (applied once or twice a year), Nutricote, and Floranid (this is similar to Triabon). Well-made compost and well-decomposed animal manure can also produce good results. Sheep pellets can be applied in a fine bark mix (for aeration) but on their own there's a danger of suffocating the surface roots. Occasional applications of dolomite will ensure calcium is supplied without altering soil pH levels. Some growers report satisfactory results with liquid fertilisers.

Be cautious with feeding: it is better to underfeed than to overdo it. Light, regular feeding is best. In the United States customers buying vireyas from retail outlets are given this simple, three-rule advice: don't overwater, don't overfeed, and don't overpot (see page 46 for advice on repotting).

WATERING. As part of their epiphytic tendency, vireyas appear to have greater drought-tolerance than other members of the genus. Dr Michael Black found one vireya growing only in 'dry crisp moss'. The water your vireyas receive might be rainwater (the best), river or pond water, bore water, chlorinated and fluoridated city supply, or a mixture of these, and all will have a bearing on plant health.

Opposite: 'Simbu Sunset'

MULCHING. This goes hand-in-hand with feeding and is especially important as vireyas have shallow root systems. Vireyas need a soil covering that is soft and well aerated. Rocks, for example, are too heavy and would prevent aeration of the roots, although small pebbles may be adequate. It's better to use organic material, such as leaf litter, bark, pine needles (which are very good), peat products, pea straw, tree-fern fibre, or garden shreddings excluding lawn clippings. Avoid also sawdust and spent mushroom compost, unless used in very small quantities in conjunction with another material. In Australia rice hulls are available and are reported to make an effective mulch. Also from Australia, a mixture of three parts pine needles and one part wood shavings has been used. And, for those who can get them, an attractive, almost permanent mulch (taking decades to decompose) can be made from macadamia nut shells. Unfortunately, most macadamia orchards find that demand exceeds supply. In future, gardeners can expect more coconut products to come from Pacific Island exporters who are promoting these manufacturing by-products as alternatives to non-renewable resources such as peat.

Alternatively, you can use a live groundcover. Lawn growing close to vireyas is not recommended, but some groundcovers are beneficial — see page 71.

Although mulching is essential for plant vitality, it's not a case of the more of it the better. Mulch should be applied wisely. Thin layers applied more often are better than an infrequent mound, for it's important not to bury the roots deeply. A mulch is only a soil cover and not a fertiliser, but all organic mulches will gradually break down to varying extents and so add to the vireyas' nutritional intake. In warm climates bacterial and fungal activity combined with the labours of worms and insects will break down a mulch more quickly than in cooler areas.

Growing vireyas in the garden

Where the soil is porous, volcanic or free-draining, vireyas can be planted at ground level. But if there's even the slightest tendency towards undue water retention, raised beds are needed. Use railway sleepers, garden edging, 'half-round' logs, rocks or tree-fern logs to raise the soil level at least 20 cm. For the soil mix, you can use any of the following: a commercial potting mix; a combination of your own soil with fine bark,

A nicely rounded bush ready to burst into flower

peat and fine scoria; compost (if it's of good quality and well balanced), bark and coarse sand; or leaf mould, tree-fern fibre and potting mix; equal parts of pumice (or perlite), potting mix and fine bark, which is a reliable formula; or any similar recipe that provides excellent aeration for the roots. Some growers report success using sawdust as a main ingredient in the mix. Even a simple mixture of fine and medium bark can be adequate. Note, though, that commercial rhododendron mixes containing acid plant food have generally proved too acidic for vireyas. Because water must be able to freely drain away, the mix shouldn't be too fine or it may become compacted and thereby exclude air from the root system.

It is crucial to plant the vireya so that the root ball is barely covered. The junction of stem and roots should be just at surface level. *Vireyas fail more often through being planted too deeply in the ground — or too deeply buried in a pot — than for any other reason.* This applies to every situation, even where soil porosity is good and there's no need for raised beds.

Dig a shallow hole or depression, gently cover the root ball just to the surface, then add a light, well-aerated layer of mulch. Don't compact the soil by giving it a hard tamping down. Vireyas are mostly surface-rooting and their fine, fibrous roots need to spread just below the soil surface where they can take up water and air; they cannot survive being deeply buried, nor can they stand having tightly packed soil around the stem. It's easy to understand this if you visualise vireyas in their natural habitat high in the trees.

Yellow 'Guilded Sunrise', bright pink 'Dr Hermann Sleumer' and softer pink 'Star Posy'

43

'Pink Delight'

Vireyas will grow perfectly well in the ground in their original plastic planter bags or in containers, provided they receive the moisture, nutrients and mulching that container-grown plants would normally receive. Of course, the soil surrounding the buried container must still be free-draining. The vireya will benefit even more if the bottom of the plastic bag is removed and if it's planted in an outer bed of vireya mix.

Another way of growing these plants, and one of the best, since it's a compromise between a container-grown plant and an in-ground one, is the tree-fern ring. Obtaining large crosscuts of tree-fern logs may be the hardest part. However, once you have your ring, preferably about 20–40 cm in diameter or any size your plant will fit into, and about 35–45 cm high, set it in the ground to one-third of its depth. After experimenting you may wish to adjust this and bury it deeper in the ground or raise it higher. Fill the ring with an appropriate mix, plant the vireya in it as you would in a container and mulch well. The mulch can be applied on top of the mix and all around the outside of the ring. Thereafter, water and feed it in the usual way. You will find that the roots don't dry out as fast as in an above-ground pot. The vireya's roots will also enjoy the confinement before eventually penetrating the encircling fibrous layer to the surface beyond.

Vireyas in containers

Apart from the fact that vireyas are supremely suited to container culture because their root systems are adapted to growing in confined spaces, growing vireyas in containers has obvious advantages.

First, portability means that you can display containers in places of prominence

44

when the plants are blooming and then relocate them at other times, replacing them with the next attraction. In cooler climates, especially where heavy frosts mean vireyas would not survive the winter, portability enables over-wintering indoors, in a shadehouse or greenhouse, or under a verandah roof.

Second, you have control over the growing medium — you can ensure that the mix is perfect. Vireyas grown in garden beds are subject to changes in soil composition, leaching, deposits from cats and dogs, and so on.

Third, you can position a container in the most suitable site available. You can protect the plants from severe heat, burning sun, or excessive wind as necessary. You can rotate or reposition a container to ensure that foliage growth is uniform, which doesn't always happen with in-ground shrubs, and you can move it to a comfortable position for repotting or pruning (easier on the back!).

Fourth, you have control over their growth. Contained roots can to some extent slow growth. And if you want to keep a plant from growing too big you can use a bonsai method of root pruning, but handle them gently.

Finally, containers are a decorator's delight. Retail garden centres exploit their attributes with swaths of containers in a huge range of sizes, materials, colours and shapes. You can experiment with matching flower colour and pot colour, with positioning plants to advantage, or arranging duplicate containers in pairs or in groups for impact. Even balcony gardeners can create a real impact with massed vireyas in modest-sized pots.

'Coral Flare' is well suited to a container

45

This hybrid makes an attractive hanging basket

Thick rather than thin pots are best for keeping the roots cool. Lighter-coloured pots will also help by reflecting more sunlight than dark-coloured containers. Above all, when choosing a container, make sure there are adequate drainage holes. If not, put scoria in the bottom of the pot when planting and raise the container on blocks above ground level. It's easy enough to check the drainage before planting by pouring a bucket of water over the filled container to ensure that the water drains away rapidly.

Vireya cultivation continues to be a matter of experiment. In contradiction to all that has been said above about the need for sharp drainage, an Australian nurseryman known for his skill with vireyas reports standing his plastic pots in a shallow pool of water for several weeks at a time (while he was away on holiday) with no ill effects. Indeed, plant health was better, he said, than when watered from above. Note that this was during hot weather only, and that the feeding roots at the surface of his tall pots (presumably) drew up moisture from the bottom, which was kept cool — cooler than the bottom of pots standing above ground.

Earthworms in pots are not usually a problem, but gardeners troubled by them can soak the container in a tub or bucket of water with dishwashing detergent at normal dishwashing strength. A 15-minute soak gets rid of earthworms while vireyas suffer no ill effects.

When repotting, resist the temptation to place a young plant into a much bigger container with the idea of providing plenty of room for future root growth. It could languish and die, as the small root system is unable to take up all the available water and nutrients, and if the mix turns sour this may cause root rot. Instead, plant the small vireya in a small pot, and put the small pot into a larger pot. Fill the rest of the outer container with coarse bark or scoria. Even with larger, older plants, it is still wise to repot only to the next size up.

A well-grown and cared-for vireya can live untroubled in the same container for many years. Except in extreme cases of neglect, vireyas do not suffer as much as other garden shrubs if they become rootbound. However, when a vireya has very obviously outgrown its pot, it should be removed and repotted into a larger container. Enmeshed roots can be gently teased apart.

When repotting, always handle the roots gently, leaving a good cover of mix clinging to the root ball. Ensure that the repotted plant is positioned so that the root ball is at the same level as previously, sprinkle over a light mulch, and avoid pressing down hard on the roots. Thoroughly moisten the mix immediately.

Hanging baskets

Baskets are brilliant! A healthy vireya in a hanging basket, with cascading shiny foliage and bursting with flowers, is a wonderful sight.

While it's important to have the right structure, lining and ingredients, it's equally important to select the right plants: some vireyas aren't suited to basket culture whereas others seem made for it.

Choose a vireya with a bushy or spreading form. Many miniature vireyas have a spreading habit, and some could even be described as weeping — perfect for baskets. Sometimes — and don't attempt this if you haven't grown vireyas in baskets before — a severe pruning can produce suitable qualities in a seemingly unsuitable plant. But usually the rule applies that if a young plant doesn't look like basket material, you can be sure the older plant won't be. In any case, with so many good, tried, spreading plants to choose from, in both miniature and medium sizes, it should be easy enough to find a plant that appeals.

Miniature hybrid 'Tom Thumb'

47

Recommended miniatures include: 'Craig Faragher', 'Alise Nicole', 'Blush Tumble', 'Carillon Bells', ' Little Ginger', 'Littlest Angel' and 'Penny Whistle'. 'Craig Faragher' has a naturally low, spreading habit and is so well suited to basket culture that one such plant is reported to be still growing and flowering happily after 15 years in the same container.

Suitable medium-sized plants for larger baskets include: *R. lochae*, 'Aravir', 'Lochmin', 'Red Rover', 'Just Peachy', 'Coral Flare', 'Fireball', 'Vladimir Bukovsky' and 'Pacific Shower'.

Wire baskets are probably the most widely used container. They can be lined with sphagnum and then filled with potting mix. Sphagnum moss is relatively inexpensive, long-lasting, it looks good in baskets, and of course its main virtue is that it holds water well. Coconut fibre, sold like cloth on-the-roll, can be used as an alternative liner to sphagnum.

In addition to wire baskets there are other hanging containers: slatted wood cubes, within which is placed a plastic pot, or perhaps the slats could be lined with weedmat; terracotta hanging pots; synthetic peat baskets; hollowed-out and shaped tree-fern containers with wire handles; woven cane baskets lined with weedmat; pottery, which may need some experimenting with; or similar pieces for which gardeners may keep an eye out when browsing in craft shops.

Use the same growing medium for baskets as for any container — for example, a mixture of pumice, potting mix and tree-fern fibre. Watering, of course, must be done conscientiously, since a plant suspended in the air will dry out more quickly than one

An unexpected combination of spring flowers with the vireya hybrid 'Littlest Angel'

'Bellendon Coral'

Hybrid miniature 'Penny Whistle'

49

'Halo hybrid'

grown in a container at ground level. On the other hand, the basket size relative to plant size is not as important as it is with on-the-ground containers, because there is less risk of waterlogging or souring of the soil. So small vireyas can be confidently planted in large baskets.

Tying down is not normally necessary because there are so many suitable varieties. However, an upright plant can occasionally be made more prostrate by tying down its outer stems to the edges of the basket. Getting the form right with the first tying is important, for thereafter the plant will grow outwards by itself.

The following suggestion is a variation on baskets, and may approximate some wild habitats. A Queensland grower, who had earlier had great success with 'Tropic Fanfare' and 'Pacific Shower' in baskets, experimented with the latter by placing it in a pouch inside a mature staghorn fern, itself an epiphyte growing on a tree in good light. He suggested peat moss or a fibrous compost as a growing medium. The idea was taken up by another Australian grower, also with 'Pacific Shower' (whose tolerance he praised for its past survival of drought, frost and near suffocation by weeds!), which had been growing in a 15 cm pot. After soaking the pot and hosing the intended host plant (an elkhorn fern), a 'nice cosy nest' was made and the vireya tucked in with composted sawdust — and there it thrived.

Pruning and shaping

The purpose of pruning is to improve the plant's shape. To produce a bushy, full-foliaged shrub, early pruning is essential. If a vireya is left to mature unpruned, it may

Opposite: 'Honey Star'

51

'Red Rooster'

'Red Rover'

grow into a leggy plant with more bare stem and less leaf cover.

Only healthy plants should be pruned; a weak plant could die as a result or produce only weak new growth. A nurseryman advises that if the cutting from which the plant was propagated came from the end of the branch, it's likely to shoot upwards. But if the growing tip had first been removed, or if the plant had been propagated from a cutting that had been taken from the second node from the tip, it is likely to send out side branches, making a better framework of branches and producing a bushy, full-foliaged plant. With the upright-growing plant, it pays to snip off the shoot tip just above the second node.

Some vireyas naturally produce two or three side shoots, others six or seven; the more produced, the bushier the plant will be. The next step is to tip prune each of these new branches, although sometimes a vireya will flower at this point, following which new shoots will develop naturally. Remove the flowers at an early stage and then wait until these new shoots are well established. The next pruning is when the plant is bigger and has produced more new foliage. Prune half of the bush and when the resulting new shoots from that half have become established, the other half can be pruned. This will promote successive flowers over a longer period.

Some growers regularly pinch out the centre of each new shoot that doesn't have a flower bud, no matter what the size of the bush, a practice they say results in more flowers as well as more leaves. If you find that your plants don't respond to this treatment, try feeding them at the same time to encourage them to produce multiple branches.

'Niugini Firebird'

53

All of this should result in a leafy, rounded shrub that's a far cry from the craggy, bare-stemmed specimens that sometimes, unfortunately, represent the group. If so pruned when young, plants will rarely need attention later.

Vireyas can also be trained as standards and the procedure for this is described on page 70.

Deadheading

Deadheading is a necessary practice to encourage new flower and leaf growth and prevent the plant diverting its energy into seed production. While the task would not seem irksome, it was for Mr J. Clyde Smith, author of the book *Vireya Rhododendrons* and editor of the Australian newsletter *Vireya Venture*. Clyde Smith's plant of 'Sunny' bloomed so spectacularly that at 1.5 m high and 1.5 m wide, it was ablaze with flowers. The flowers were so numerous and the task of deadheading them so tiresome that to relieve the boredom he 'counted the trusses as they were removed and the total was 862, each with an average of some four flowers' per truss. Could anyone ask for more?

Hardening Off

Young plants sold at nurseries and garden centres are normally hardened off. But if you've obtained plants grown in a protected environment under full shade where they appear to grow in peak condition, you may find that on planting them in the garden they appear to sicken. This happens if they've not been acclimatised. The younger

'Shepherds Warning'

the plant, the more vulnerable it is, which is why the best plant to buy is an older one.

How can you tell if a plant has been acclimatised? Look for hardened stems and foliage. Rigidity and possibly paleness of leaf mean the plant has had some exposure to less sheltered conditions; an overall soft, tender appearance may indicate that it hasn't. In those cultivars which naturally have a red pigment in the leaves and stems, the red coloration should be already apparent. The advice to 'look for a hardened appearance' may not seem helpful, but with practice it becomes easier to spot. If you feel you really can't tell, ask the nursery staff.

To harden a plant, start by exposing it to the sun, wind and rain gradually for just an hour or two at a time. Gradually increase the exposure time over a period of four or five weeks, after which they should be fully adjusted to the outdoor environment.

Plant Disorders

Weak plants are more susceptible to problems than healthy ones — a familiar refrain, but true.

INSECTS.The only insects likely to cause trouble are thrips, mealy bugs and mites, which will infest weak rather than healthy plants. The best remedy for such problems is to water, feed and mulch the plants into good health. Give the foliage regular syringing with water. If these microscopic pests persist, try spraying a mild solution of insecticide and oil; if the outbreak is minor, use just oil. A miticide is required for mites, which are related to spiders rather than true insects. Larger bugs don't seem to bother vireyas. Aphids and scale insects are never a problem, although sometimes leafroller caterpillars will attack the leaves of certain species, such as *R. goodenoughii* or *R. stenophyllum*.

DISEASES. Thankfully, vireyas are generally free from disease, however mildew, both powdery and downy, is occasionally a problem. It seems to occur in hybrids of *R. lochae* or *R. konori* parentage and appears more often on container-grown plants during dry weather. Weak or stressed plants are always vulnerable. Treat with a fungus and mildew spray.

RUST. Rust appears as bright orange spots clustered on the reverse side of the leaves, and in extreme cases on the stems and upper leaf surface. Caught in its early stages it can be remedied by removing all the affected leaves and burning them. If the problem persists it may be necessary to use a fungicide — or dig out the whole plant and burn it. ('Princess Alexander', a Veitch hybrid, is one of only a few vireyas likely to be troubled by rust.)

LEAF SPOT. Reddish leaf spots can sometimes indicate a magnesium deficiency. This is remedied by applications of epsom salts. Spots that sometimes occur in winter may be caused by cold, wet weather. They are not really a problem and always go away again in spring. The cultivar 'Cameo Spice' seems noticeably susceptible to leaf spot.

LEGGY GROWTH. Some species and hybrids are naturally leggy — *R. leucogigas, R. laetum* and *R. aurigeranum*, for example. With others a bushier habit can be induced

'Kisses'

by pruning. This is is best done at a young age before the plant has had a chance to shoot upwards (see page 53).

BUD DIEBACK. A few known instances of terminal dieback of both leaf and flower buds have been attributed to boron deficiency. A soluble fertiliser containing trace elements remedied the problem. Once again, healthy well-nourished plants shouldn't suffer this affliction.

SICKLY FOLIAGE. Sometimes vireya leaves appear in poor health for no apparent reason, so close examination of the whole plant is necessary.

Firstly make sure that the plant is not planted too deeply and that the roots are well-aerated, mulched and have adequate moisture and nutrients. Above all, make sure that water drains away freely. Check the undersides of the leaves for thrips or rust. A plant suffering from excessive heat can also look ill. Where summers are hot and humid the best strategy is to grow only those hybrids whose parentage can be traced to low altitudes.

LEAF DROP. The best way to encourage new leaf growth is to prune, but don't do this during hot dry periods when leaf drop may occur. Ensure that the plant has a plentiful supply of moisture and feed it back into good health, and prune only then. Bushy new growth should result.

FLOWER WILT. Pollination by bees is often the cause of flower wilt. Another cause might be sun; strong, full-day sun during the height of summer can be enough to cause newly opened flower trusses to wilt. Relocate the plant if it's in a container, or

provide a temporary screen to shield it from the sun — especially the mid-afternoon sun — and give the plant a thorough watering in the evening or early morning.

SPLIT FLOWERS. From time to time a quite widespread incidence of flowers opening with split corollas occurs. Most growers don't mind. The cause is uncertain but one theory is that splitting results from cold, overcast weather followed by sudden warmth. It is also thought that one or two hybrids may have a genetic tendency to produce split flowers, in which case there's no remedy other than to discard the plant.

FROST DAMAGE. Frost damage varies according to the cold tolerance of each different species and hybrid. Those species originating in the highest altitudes, and hybrids derived from them, are naturally better suited to growing in climates with frosty winters. Other than careful selection at the time of purchase, it's advisable to start with older, mature plants rather than young ones, avoiding soft tender plants that have not been hardened off adequately. Mature plants are less likely to be damaged by frost; if they are in containers they can be moved to a sheltered situation during the high-risk months. If you do grow them in the ground outside, make sure they're in raised beds and in the sun rather than the shade. Plants grown in this manner will suffer less than plants left outside in containers.

Take heart, too, in the knowledge that light frost damage can actually benefit your plants. Think of it as a form of light pruning from which they may burst out in spring with renewed vigour. On the whole, light frosts do no harm, but heavy frost can be fatal.

'Vladimir Bukovsky'

Propagation

The two main methods of propagation are by seed and by cuttings. Other methods such as layering, grafting and tissue culture are likely to be of more interest to the commercial grower than the home gardener.

The technique used will depend on your aims and the plant concerned. Hybirds are the result of crossing two genetically distinct parents and because of their mixed parentage will not come true from seed — that is, the seedlings will be variable rather than identical to the original plant. So to perpetuate hybrids, plants must be propagated vegetatively, and cuttings are the simplest method. Seed collected from hybrids can be used but only if you are interested in obtaining new forms. Vireyas are self-fertile and if hybrids are self-pollinated, genetic recombination should result in a range of variation among the progeny.

Species normally come true from seed so long as cross-pollination with a different species or hybrid has not occurred, although there is still likely to be minor variation among the offspring. But a particularly good clone of a species should be propagated vegetatively, as seedlings from it may be inferior.

Seed

The viability of vireya seed is limited. The seed of some species remains viable for only three or four weeks, so it's important to sow it as soon as possible after harvesting.

Ripened seed can be spread on finely sifted peat or other organic matter so long as the medium has been sterilised. The seed should be left uncovered. The optimum temperature for germination is 22–25°C. Water it lightly and partially cover the container with glass or clear plastic, or instead use regular misting to keep the mix damp. Light is not necessary for germination; after germination it can be gradually increased.

Be patient. Germination time varies with temperature, seed-storage time, and with each variety, but usually seeds germinate within one to three weeks. (While fresh seed is the best guarantee of results, an American collector, Bill Moyles, has successfully stored chilled seed for over two years.)

Germination can be very slow. When the infant vireyas are 2 cm high they are ready to be pricked out into little pots containing peat or fine bark and perlite. Pot them in groups of four or five or more. Liquid fertiliser at a very dilute strength can be given at this stage and weekly thereafter. When the seedlings are 5–6 cm tall they will be 'fully fledged' and can be potted up separately.

While seed germination may seem an endlessly slow process compared with propagation by cuttings, it is through pollination by hand that new hybrids are created, and with results that can be well worth the wait. This is how most of today's colourful galaxy of hybrids were created.

From seedling to flowering can be as short as two years for some, and as long as 10–15 years for others.

Cuttings

Propagation by cuttings is easier and faster. Internodal cuttings can be taken at any time of the year from both old and new stems. It may pay to give the intended donor bushes a light feeding several months before taking the cuttings. The cuttings should be about 15 cm and taken from firm terminal shoots. Remove all the lower leaves so that the number is reduced by about half, then trim the remaining leaves by half — this makes the cutting easier to handle and reduces water stress on the cutting. At this stage some growers (those willing to use toxic chemicals) wash the cuttings in a fungicide such as Benlate to reduce the risk of root rot. There are safer alternatives to Benlate, such as bleach at the rate of a few teaspoons to a gallon of water. The base of each cutting is then wounded, a process akin to sharpening a pencil, by removing thin slivers from the basal 1–2 cm of the stem. This exposes more of the underlying cambium layer, the area from which the new roots will develop. Often the wounded bases are then dipped in rooting hormone to augment root growth, although they'll still root without the hormone dip, but with probably a lower percentage of success. Plant the cuttings in a mix of fine peat and perlite or a similar mix, and take care that it doesn't dry out. Place the container in a well-lit situation but out of direct sunlight. Ensure the cuttings are correctly labelled.

Commercial horticulturalists and vireya growers in the northern hemisphere who aim for a maximum strike rate systematically use bottom heat. However, most amateur propagators will find that their cuttings will root satisfactorily without bottom heat. The tops should be kept cool by misting regularly.

Rooting may take up to ten weeks, at which time they can be moved to a less sheltered area with more air circulation still away from direct sunlight. Dilute liquid fertiliser can be applied at this stage. Then, in another few weeks they can be potted up.

'Cameo Spice'

60

Growing vireyas indoors

In those parts of the United States and Canada where winters are severe, vireyas are successfully grown outdoors in summer in containers which are moved inside for the winter. In milder areas, such as the southeast USA and southern California, they can grow in the garden all year round. There are also intermediate areas. Northern California, for example, offers mild microclimates with mostly frost-free conditions which allow for outside culture but where gardeners still need to be wary of the exceptional freeze that can come sweeping down from the Arctic. Their response at such times is to provide temporary frost protection until the threat has passed.

But for vireya growers in Oregon, Washington, British Columbia and, of course, all of the central and northeastern states of the USA where containered plants must over-winter indoors, these observations by experienced growers may be helpful.

Potting mix
The most commonly used mix in North America consists of one part pumice or perlite and one part bark/peat. Sometimes a polymer is used to help the water-holding capacity of the mix. Shredded redwood bark collected from the coast of northern California has been tried successfully, although reportedly the plants later appeared reluctant to adapt to a change of mix. Even shredded styrofoam has been tried — with poor results — along with other ingredients. The tree-fern fibre that works so well for Australian and New Zealand growers is not readily available in the USA.

Fertiliser
Liquid fertiliser applied at quarter- to half-strength is recommended; never use full strength. Apply once a year on young plants, and after they are two years old and have developed a root system, apply three or four times a year. Plants which spend part of the year indoors seem to do best with liquid, rather than granule, feeding, though this is not a firm rule. Natural organic fertilisers such as cotton seed meal or alfalfa meal may need to be augmented with trace elements.

Indoor temperatures
Plants must not freeze. They should be kept at temperatures above freezing point (0°C or 32°F) and have proved surprisingly tolerant of cool temperatures just above freezing. However most indoor temperatures are warmer than this — around 55°–75°F — and this seems to suit vireyas as an average indoor daytime temperature. It is

important that night-time temperatures be lower that daytime temperatures — about 40°F. In Tecoma, near Seattle, a collection of about a hundred very healthy vireyas spend the winter in a small, plastic, lean-to shed. This plant house is lined with clear plastic and heated with a small oil heater with the thermostat set to a temperature of just above 32°F (0°C). It is cheap and effective.

Ensuring indoor plant health

Give your vireyas as much light as you can. The longer the winter, the more important it is to give them maximum light. During this over-wintering period watering should be just enough and no more — enough to prevent stress. Never over-water. To quote from the cultivation advice of Bovees Nursery in Portland, Oregon, 'Don't *keep* your plant dry, just let it *become* dry and then water.' Similarly, keep applications of fertiliser to a minimum. Perhaps use very dilute liquid fertiliser or rely on just the residual nutrients left from a slow-release fertiliser applied the previous spring.

Ventilation

Because vireyas in the wild grow epiphytically, often high in canopies, it's easy to assume that high levels of air movement are essential. Yet the adaptable vireya survives surprisingly well indoors with restricted ventilation. It may be necessary to experiment with indoor locations to ensure that ventilation is adequate.

Plant disorders

Indoor vireyas provided with the above conditions don't usually suffer from pests or diseases. As always, it's important to be vigilant, and early gatherings of insects on leaves can be quickly rubbed off or removed by hand. In extreme cases it may be necessary to spray. Don't despair if plants show very little growth during winter. It is natural that in areas with darker, longer winters plant growth will slow down.

Moving plants outdoors

Once the weather begins warming, your vireyas can be moved outside. It is vital that indoor vireyas be 'hardened off' first; that is, exposed only gradually to outside conditions. This is because their indoor period makes them 'soft' and they are less able to cope with changes in their environment. Once winter is over, don't heave armloads of pots out into the middle of a lawn and leave them where they'll suffer from shock; instead, put them outside by the shelter of a wall or hedge and only for a few hours at a time each day. Slowly give them more and more direct light. Morning sun is preferable to noon and afternoon sun. Protect them from drying winds. You'll learn to 'read' your plants and will see them hardening up. While the extent of this vulnerability varies from one plant to another, unless you're very experienced and can read the signs, it pays to treat all vireyas to this process of exposure by degrees.

Flowering

Vireyas will bloom successfully indoors and out. Some growers have observed that indoor winter flowering (a good showing-off time!) may follow a pattern whereby bud-set occurs at the 12-hour day cycle in autumn (and is repeated outdoors following

An array of hybrids grown under cover: 'Pink Delight',
'Tashbaan', 'Buttermilk', 'Aravir' and 'Pink Ray'

'Liberty Bar' growing indoors with potted
plants including *Cycas revoluta*

the spring 12-hour day period). E. White Smith, editor of the *Vireya Vine* newsletter, believes that 12-hour days trigger bud-set for two reasons: '. . . one because the temperature differences are more pronounced, and the other is the fact that in their native habitat they normally live in a + or - 12-hour day all year round.'

Growing vireyas indoors year round

In summer the threat to vireyas grown indoors is excessive heat. Provided the plants have adequate light, moisture and feeding, they can be grown in glasshouses or shade-houses or anywhere else where there is good ventilation to avoid heat build up. The importance of ventilation increases with increased temperatures. Commercial glasshouses usually have a system of vents which are opened as well as electrically operated fans to circulate the air. Collectors and those with large numbers of vireyas may prefer to keep their plants housed year round, but for most home gardeners — even those with limited outdoor space — the gradual move outdoors is easily accomplished.

Once outdoors, plants often have growth spurts. Spring and early summer is the time for increased watering, fertilising and repotting as necessary.

Landscaping with vireyas

The most valuable attribute of vireyas in the landscape is their versatility. Their form, which can be both predicted and controlled, offers the landscaper structure and substance. Where gaps need filling, particularly between ground level and the canopy, their foliage fills vertical voids. With their preference for half-shade, and the tolerance of some varieties for near full-shade, they have particular value. As standards displayed individually in formal settings, they can be arresting. And as companion plants in existing gardens, they blend splendidly with many other shrubs, bulbs of every kind (especially the fiery-hued *Hippeastrum* and other Amaryllidaceae), box hedges, groundcovers and climbers, as well as with many perennials and annuals — companions all.

The carefully planned and designed garden, though, is not for everyone. Enthusiastic collectors are less likely to be interested in the vireya's design potential and more likely to be intent on accumulation. Collectors do, of course, fulfil important roles, particularly in the late twentieth century as the world's botanical and biological gene pool is eroded, and those who nurture both species and hybrid vireyas provide an acknowledged service. But the average residential gardener who seeks visual and decorative unity is better governed by some observance of the rules of design.

Designing a garden with vireyas

First, consider the overall area of the garden and its uses. Small-sized yards are nowadays more common than large gardens and will in future be increasingly so. Contemporary gardens into which the house extends in a livable, indoor-outdoor blend provide the perfect accommodation for container-grown vireyas. They can be repositioned and regrouped with ease. Their portability enables the gardener to take advantage of local climate, rainfall, sun, shade and seasonal extremes. Standard vireyas grown in containers can be striking when standing alone. Against a background of green foliage, one standard vireya in flower makes a stunning focal point.

In small walled or fenced gardens where space is extremely limited, vireyas can be considered as drapery, as background dressing for the forecourt — the idea being to create a textured wall of strong green foliage which is layered and repeated. In this, or indeed in any planting plan, be cautious with selection. Don't buy vireyas solely for their flower colour but select instead for their overall shape, dimensions and foliage:

Opposite: Vireyas provide useful highlights in a predominantly foliage garden

think of flowers as a bonus. (Such advice may be hard to heed in the face of a cluster of scented and ravishing flowers!)

In larger gardens, vireyas can be used to colonise under palms and other trees whose canopy allows some sunlight to penetrate. For the luxuriant, tropical garden style to which vireyas are eminently suited, they can be the understorey plants to provide smaller-leafed background foliage to heighten the effect of massive-leafed specimen plants. In these tropical — or 'tamed-jungle' — gardens, the multi-purpose vireya is now established as an integral player, blending into neutrality as a foil for other plants, or as structural elements on their own. Importantly, they lend themselves by association to a far wider range of plants than the range associated with, for example, a Christmas fir or a desert cactus.

Vireyas not only fulfil the underplanting role, but can at the same time be themselves underplanted. Even the most prostrate vireyas, which spill downwards when grown in hanging baskets, are not really ground hugging and cannot be trimmed or clipped into subservience the way some newly purpose-bred shrubs (such as miniature camellias) can be trained to stay at heel. So it is at this intermediate level that vireyas have the most to offer. Choose with restraint. From a design point of view, it's better to grow a lot of a few different vireyas, rather than many different ones. And a footnote from a professional landscape architect: 'Grow vireyas well — or not at all'.

Companion plants

New Zealand gardeners are fortunate in having at hand an indigenous flora that is rich in evergreen foliage and which displays the vireya's jewel-like flowers to fine effect.

It makes a lively tapestry. Vireya leaves blend beautifully with *Pseudopanax* or puka

The pure white flowers of *R. tuba* light up a dark corner

66

(*Meryta sinclairii*) leaves; they contrast with the rough fibre of tree-fern trunks; they arch above the slender straps of the low clumping, blueberry-bearing *Dianella nigra*. Their flowers are similarly offset. There is an undeniable affinity between New Zealand's native plants and the flora of New Guinea and parts of Borneo and Indonesia which enhances the intense colours of vireya flowers, especially those fiery lights of the hot spectrum. Even white, cream and pastel shades are made buoyant by a lush backdrop that seems to recede in order that these pearls might gleam.

Foliage plants with glossy leaves that are at home in the New Zealand forest are equally at home in the vireya garden: *Griselinia lucida*, *Meryta sinclairii*, *Pisonia brunoniana*, *Coprosma repens*, *Pseudopanax arboreus*, *P. ferox*, *P.* 'Gold Splash', *Solanum* spp., *Corynocarpus laevigatus*, *Entelea arborescens*, *Macropiper excelsum*, and the robust, waxy-leafed climber *Tecomanthe speciosa*.

Within the native floras of Australia, North America, and other countries will be found similarly endowed plants with qualities that make them good vireya companions. They are worth seeking out. Choose small trees that are not shallow-rooted or ravenous feeders and whose overhead shade is partial rather than complete. Evergreen shrubs with compact, dense and dark leaves may also be suitable. Plant selection is a matter of experimenting.

The hybrid 'Coral Flare' is admirably sited in this lush rainforest-style garden.

'Java Light'   'Silken Shimmer'

Tree ferns are true allies. Planted with vireyas, young tree ferns share similar dimensions, then as they grow and overtake the vireyas they provide useful shade. At maturity they provide a high canopy. Upright posts made from felled trunks are useful for shelter and can provide hitching places for vireyas in baskets. Embedded tree-fern rings or cross-cut slices which encircle the roots but have no floor are the ideal low-maintenance container. Dead tree-fern stumps and prostrate logs are all good nesting places — just carve out a cavity and plant the vireya in it. Some of the best tree fern species to grow are *Cyathea dealbata*, the silver fern; *C. smithii*, a smaller New Zealand species for cooler locations; *C. cunninghamii*, a fast grower; the Lord Howe Island species, *C. robusta*; the very reliable *C. cooperii*; *Dicksonia squarrosa*; and *D. fibrosa*, which has a very thick brown trunk. A wonderfully elegant and desirable cyathea to grow with vireyas, but which is not readily obtainable at present, is the 'Highland lace' cyathea, *C. tomentosissima*, native to New Guinea.

Among lower-growing ferns the feathery-textured aspleniums (such as *A. bulbiferum*, *A. oblongifolium* and *A. haurakiensis*), the magnificent king fern (*Marattia salicina*) and a host of blechnums, easy-care doodias and pteris ferns are all attractive. But As a general rule, all ferns go well with vireyas.

Palms also have a natural affinity with vireyas. Like tree ferns, palms bring to gardens a touch of the exotic, of rainforests, tropical islands or far-away places . Although slower growing than tree ferns they are worth the wait. Among those popularly grown are *Trachycarpus fortunei*, *Chamaedorea*, *Archontophoenix*, *Howea forsteriana*, *Butia*, *Syagrus*, *Phoenix reclinata*, *P. roebelinii*, and *P. dactylifera*, and *Rhopalostylis sapida*, although the related *R. baueri* is considerered the more graceful.

Ferns and palms create a lush landscape into which gardeners can slip their vireya plants and know that the formula will work. The vireyas' foliage will blend into the greenery; in bloom, the flowers will shimmer. A colour scheme of yellow and yellow-orange might include the following vireyas: 'Haloed Gold', 'Ra', 'Wattlebird', 'Satans

Opposite: Planted under a *Radermacheria* tree, this hybrid suits its setting

The artistic arrangement of this small courtyard shows a vireya hybrid in a
purpose-made cavity within the paving

Gift', *R. laetum*, 'Flamenco Dancer', or 'Simbu Sunset'. A pink arrangement could
combine 'Star Posy', 'Pink Delight', 'Hot Gossip', 'Christopher John', 'Raspberry
Truffle' and 'Silken Shimmer'.

Beyond ferns and palms, the rainforest image can be extended to include other
jungle-type flora: orchids, bromeliads, dracaenas, cycads, bamboos, gingers (but not
the invasive ones), and many members of the Araceae family such alocasias, *Monstera
deliciosa*, spathiphyllums, philodendrons, and the huge *Xanthosoma*. These lush-
leafed aroids have the advantage of being fast growers.

Although gardens landscaped with these plants are undoubtedly successful, such
plants are not for every gardener and certainly not for every climate. One question
that is likely to be asked by many browsers who pick up this book is, 'Do vireyas go
with roses?' The answer is, some do and some don't. For the picket-fence and lavender

70

devotee, for the occasional-but-not-dedicated suburban gardener, and for those passionate purists who grow only old roses, here are some suggestions.

Choose miniature and small-sized vireyas with flowers in pastel shades. Select forms that do well in baskets and grow them in containers around the garden, or hang them in the company of other basket plants. Pastel colours are easy to work with; bright colours may need more planning. A bold colour scheme using orange, for example, might go with an existing blue one. If you have a lot of blue and blue-purple flowers in the garden, such as salvias, anchusas or cornflowers, choose vireyas for contrast in equally strong shades of orange, but stick to only clear oranges and no other. Don't introduce other colours. Pure orange vireyas include 'Java Light', 'Narnia', 'Sir George Holford', 'Cordial Orange', and 'Vladimir Bukovsky'.

Similarly, if the existing garden already has perennials and plants in borders that you intend keeping, choose a single-coloured vireya that is compatible with your colour scheme and plant lots of it. The repetition will unify the garden. This might be an opportunity to concentrate on fragrance, for so many gorgeous vireyas also have gorgeous scent.

If roses predominate, don't use vireya flowers to compete; instead use them to blend in. It may be best to keep large shrub roses and vireyas segregated, but small and miniature roses can happily mix with the smaller vireyas, such as 'Star Posy', 'Pink Delight', 'Little Kisses', 'Aravir', 'Silver Thimbles', 'Craig Faragher', *R. jasminiflorum*, or 'Little Ginger'. Aim for soft, wafting or trailing effects. Another

A mixed planting that includes the hybrid 'Buttermaid'

71

Grasses and similar foliage plants such as *Phormium* species and cultivars are a
good foil for vireyas

72

Bulbs

Alstroemeria; all members of the Amaryllidaceae, especially belladonna lilies (*Amaryllis*), clivias (much recommended by landscapers), crinums, *Eucomis*, *Haemanthus coccineus*, *Hippeastrum*, *Hymenocallis* and nerines; and many others, including *Crocosmia*, *Dietes* and libertias (especially *L. grandiflora* and *L. peregrinans*).

Climbing vines

Climbing plants are best used as a backdrop for vireyas rather than grown alongside them, especially in mild warm climates where their rampant growth could seize neighbouring vireyas in a throttlehold. In cooler climates this is less of a threat. Consider, with caution, the following vines for the vireya garden: *Asarina barclaiana*, *Bomarea multiflora*, *Cobaea scandens*, the Carolina jasmine (*Gelsemium sempervirens*), some of the Australian kennedias, *Lapageria rosea*, *Lonicera* (especially *L.* x *brownii* 'Dropmore Scarlet' and possibly *L. hildebrandtiana*), mandevillas, and some of the more modest-growing passion vines (*Passiflora*). One delectable climbing bulb of gentle disposition is *Gloriosa superba*. Winter dormant, its spidery, flame-coloured flowers harmonise beautifully with vireyan colours.

Standards

Do consider growing vireyas as standards. A sturdy, well-grown standard in good health and full flower can be very elegant. Landscape architects make use of them to strengthen design structure and in the company of topiaried plants standard vireyas fortify formality. To create a standard, select a cultivar that is tall and slow to flower. Compact vireyas make good standards but as these often tend to be low growing, careful selection is required. One cultivar that is outstanding as a standard is 'Charming Valentino'. Other possibilities include 'Ivory Coast', 'Popcorn', 'Little Pinkie', 'Rosie Posie', 'Pink Delight' and the species *R. loranthiflorum*.

Ensure that the main upright shoot tip has not previously been pruned, because that growing tip is vital. Ignore side branches and concentrate on vertical growth. The upright growing stem doesn't have to be ram-rod straight, just make sure it's aesthetically pleasing. One way of promoting vertical growth is to grow several standards close together like a pine forest. The closeness will encourage them to grow upwards towards the light. Be patient — standards aren't produced overnight. Keep in mind the ultimate height you are aiming for (which will vary from plant to plant) and as it grows taller and stronger, remove any side shoots starting from the bottom up. After it has reached the height you want, simple pruning is all that is required to maintain the desired shape, but be vigilant in maintaining plant health.

Underplanting with groundcovers

While standards stand alone, shrub vireyas congregate and they may eventually become quite large. The vireya that started off as an underplant for a tree fern soon becomes the middle storey under which you can plant smaller plants such as groundcovers.

Opposite: A vibrant colour combination: the climber *Thunbergia grandiflora* twining through the vireya hybrid *lochae* x *javanicum*

Hybrid 'Little Bo Peep' as a container-grown standard

Spreading and low-growing groundcovers can act as a moisture-retentive mulch. Provided their roots are not tenacious and they don't rob the ground of too many nutrients, such plants can play an important role in the design and colour scheme of a garden while at the same time contributing to the vireyas' well-being. The dainty little New Zealand fern, *Blechnum pennamarina*, can fill this role. So also can *Lamium* 'White Nancy', which makes a lively underplanting for vireyas with white flowers. *Ajuga* is ideal; *A. reptans* is soft-rooted and its deep purplish foliage looks wonderful under vireyas. Ornamental tradescantias, such as *T. pallida* or the more tropical forms, are similar in their ground-covering habits, for their roots never penetrate deeper than the top few centimetres of the soil, making them easy to pull up, and in hot positions they keep the soil cool. A better choice might be the *Ophiopogon* cultivars, which are clumping, grass-like perennials about 12 cm in height that grow well in partial shade. As a groundcover for vireyas they are among the best. The green-leafed form 'Kyoto' forms a lush carpet, but the black-leafed form 'Ebony Knight' is more dramatic. Landscapers today use it to wonderful effect.

Perhaps in future vireyas will be grown with more flair: more innovative ideas may come. Indeed, there is far more scope for flair and originality with these plants than the temperate rhododendrons have offered. There might even be scope for combining vireyas with succulents, or introducing them into an all-succulent landscape. Of course, these plants have respectively different cultivation requirements, but perhaps they could be accommodated. Or, enlarging on the use of *Ophiopogon* as a suggested groundcover, a garden composed of nothing but clumping plants — straps and spikes and grass tufts, such as variegated *Carex* or *Pennisetum setaceum*, palm grass, arundo reeds, small bamboos and astelias — could make an attractive setting for mass plantings of large vireyas. More could be made of the epiphytic preferences of vireyas by planting them on stumps, boulders and decaying logs, and emphasing height with vertical planting. The Brazilian wall plantings of Roberto Burle Marx could set an example.

It may be helpful too, to read descriptions of the species occurring naturally alongside vireyas in the wild (see Vireyas in the Wild and also the list of publications in the appendix) to further explore these ideas. In Bako National Park in Borneo for example, vireyas grow alongside pitcher plants, in addition to the usual ferns, palms and cycads. Hundreds and thousands of these insectivorous plants, *Nepenthes hookeriana*, have been recorded there enlivening the landscape in colours of red, cream and green.

A word about planting under trees: no garden arrangement ever remains static and as trees grow larger and taller, the conditions which once suited vireyas may change. In time, the shade may become too dense, air circulation may be reduced, or invasive tree roots may compete for nutrients or take up all the moisture. It may therefore become necessary to relocate your vireyas. Fortunately they're highly relocatable. They're best moved during damp weather or after a good penetrating rain. Large specimens moved to a new site may need staking for a while. Vireyas are so moveable, so versatile and their flowers so full of surprises and joy, that such changes often bring further enhancement.

'Christopher John'

A poolside planting of 'Java Light'

The focus of this chapter has been more on plants grown in the garden than in containers. But one setting that is almost devoid of garden is the sparse lines and clear surfaces of the uncluttered courtyard, the outdoor living spaces of contemporary townhouses and apartments, where there may be are no green backdrops and where paving and containers may be the only features. Here, too, the vireya excels. The reflective surfaces and the absence of lawn and other areas of vegetation may mean that more care is called for in fulfilling their cultivation needs, but in terms of the visual effect, vireyas in artificial spaces can dazzle.

For the ultimate patio presentation, put containers of bold vireyas in bloom next to a swimming pool. Swimming pools are usually coloured blue or deep slate, and beside them the bewitching vireyan colours make a compelling combination. Water is associated with cool calm emotions, while the vireyas' vibrant colours sing of sun and heat — a mix most people find irresistible. Even ornamental pools and fish ponds look marvellous with their edges garnished with potted vireyas. If you want a quieter colour arrangement — something more soothing — container-grown vireyas in soft salmon, white, cream or lemon shades may be your choice.

Reliable beginners' plants — proven performers
'Pink Delight', 'Coral Flare', 'First Light', 'Tropic Glow', 'Sweet Wendy', 'St Valentine', 'Simbu Sunset', 'Cherry Pie', 'Just Peachy', 'Sunny Splendour', 'Kisses', 'Satan's Gift', 'Vladimir Bukovsky', 'Littlest Angel', 'Aravir', 'Pacific Sundown', 'Brightly', 'George Budgen', 'Gilded Sunrise', 'Elizabeth Ann Seton'.

Handsome foliage
'Dresden Doll', 'Cyprian', 'Bold Janus', 'Gardenia Odyssey', 'Hugh Redgrove', 'Bob's Crowning Glory', 'Charming Valentino', 'Golden Charm', 'Peach Dream', 'Cordial Orange', 'Magic Flute', 'Blushed Spice'.

Scented vireyas
'Christopher John', 'Cameo Spice', 'Aravir', 'Gardenia Odyssey', *R. loranthiflorum*, 'Jean Baptiste', 'Arne Jensen', 'Humboldt Bay', 'Bob's Crowning Glory', 'Great Scent-sation', 'Gwenevere', 'Dr Herman Sleumer' (and hybrids), 'Moonwood', 'Satan's Gift', 'Peach Dream', 'Cherry Liqueur', 'Cecilia', 'Cream Delight', 'Buttermilk', 'Marshall Pierce Madison', 'Bernadette'.

Tall
'Halo Gold', 'Calavar', 'Bold Janus', 'Wattlebird', 'Gilded Sunrise', Halo hybrid series, 'Toff', 'Hari's Choice', 'Sweet Amanda'.

Medium bushy
'George Budgen', 'Honey Star', 'Pacific Sundown', 'Popcorn', 'Rosie Posie', 'Apricot Gem', 'Fireplum', 'Lemon Light', 'Ivory Coast', 'Pink Rory'.

Low and spreading
'Red Rover', 'Show Stopper', 'Highland Arabesque', 'Fireball', 'Just Peachy', 'Lochmin', 'Bronze Warrior', 'Golden Casket', 'Flamingo Bay', 'Pacific Shower', 'Magic Flute'.

Shade-tolerant
'Brightly', 'Pink Ray', 'Pretty Cotton Candy', 'Simbu Sunset', 'Liberty Bar', 'First Light', 'Popcorn', 'Christopher John', 'Just Peachy'.

Sun-tolerant
'Stanton's Glory', 'Arthur's Choice', 'Cyprian', 'Buttermaid', 'Niugini Firebird', 'Toff', 'Sunny Splendour', 'Cape Cod Sunshine', 'Java Light', 'Apricot Gem'.

Colours
WHITE: 'Popcorn', 'Aravir', 'Gwenevere', 'Jean Baptiste', *loranthiflorum*, 'Gossamer White'.
PINK: 'Pendance', 'Star Posy', 'Pink Seedling', 'Shaya', 'Little Pinkie', 'Gossamer Pink'.
APRICOT: 'Tashbaan', 'Apricot Charm', 'Harry Wu', 'Bold Janus', 'Maid Marion'.
ORANGE: 'Bronze Warrior', 'Brightly', 'Cordial', 'Java Light', 'Vladimir Bukovsky'.
YELLOW-GOLD: 'Goldilocks', 'Buttermaid', 'Wattlebird', 'Golden Casket', *R. laetum*, 'Anarta Gold'.
RED: 'Fireball', 'Red Rooster', 'Chimbu Glow', 'Hot Gossip', 'Hari's Choice', 'Ne Plus Ultra'.

Where to see and buy vireyas

Selected public gardens featuring vireyas

New Zealand
Eden Gardens
Omana Avenue
Mt Eden
Auckland

Pukeiti Rhododendron Trust
New Plymouth

Australia
Australian Rhododendron Society
Mt Pleasant
Wollongong
NSW

Botanic Gardens
Adelaide
South Australia

National Rhododendron Garden
Olinda
Victoria

USA
Strybing Arboretum
San Francisco
California

UCLA Botanic Garden
California

American Rhododendron Society
P.O. Box 1380
Gloucester, VA 23061

Lyon Arboretum
Honolulu
Hawaii

Scotland
Edinburgh Botanic Gardens
Edinburgh

Vireya nurseries

New Zealand

Koromiko Nursery
RD 9
Whangarei

J. & B. Oldham
102 Meadowbank Road
Meadowbank
Auckland

D & P Brown
Vernon Road
Te Puna, Tauranga

Te Puna Cottage Gardens
245 Te Puna Road
RD 6
Tauranga

Jurys Nursery
PO Box 65
Urenui, North Taranaki

Pukeiti Rhododendron Trust
New Plymouth

Woodleigh Nursery
Oakura
New Plymouth

Australia

Rhodo Glen Nurseries
6 Georges Road
The Patch
Victoria

Rosemont Nurseries
960 Mount Dandenong Tourist Road
Victoria

Vireya Valley Nursery
Woori-Yallock Road
Cockatoo, Victoria

Warran Glen Nurseries
373 Warrandyte Road
Victoria

Sapersteins Nursery
Main Arm
Mullumbimby, NSW
 (wholesale only)

The Vireya Venue
2 Clifford Street
Maleny, Queensland 4552

USA

Bovees Nursery
(publisher of *Vireya Vine* quarterly newsletter)
1737 SW Coronado
Portland, OR 97219

Greer Gardens
1280 Goodpasture Island Road
Eugene, OR 97401

Red's Rhodies
15920 SW Oberst Lane
Sherwood, OR 97140

Cape Cod Vireyas
405 Jones Road
Falmouth, MA

Rhododendron Species Botanic Garden
PO Box 3798
Federal Way
WA 98003

Vireya hybrids and species

Normal practice in botanical referencing is to list species before hybrids. Here the order is reversed. With vireyas, hybrids are (in general) easier to grow. Their performance in the home garden is more reliable, and their flowering often more spectacular than that of species.

The hybrid selection that follows is based upon all-round attributes which include growth habit, hardiness, vigour, ease of cultivation, shrub size and shape, quality of foliage, flower shape, flower size and colour, scent, and flowering frequency. The list includes plants grown in Australia, New Zealand, the United States and a few from the United Kingdom. They are not all available in any one country.

Almost all of the plants in the first list are hybrids; the only species included are those which have proved to be adaptable and easily grown.

'Alisa Nicole'. Although a miniature, the bell flowers in plum-pink are surprisingly large for such a small plant. This is a good pot or basket plant and is almost always in bloom.

'Anastasia'. A dependable bloomer, this is a small to medium upright bush with shiny green leaves and hanging trusses of waxy red flowers.

'Anggi Lake'. Slow-growing, many-branched and compact, this reliable hybrid has rounded leaves in dark olive-green, and large, tubular-flared flowers in clear pink, with pale pink to white tubes.

'Annata Gold'. This vireya has good sun-tolerance. The rippled flowers are large and shaded in deep gold with sienna throats.

'Apricot Charm'. A bushy, spreading shrub, this container or garden vireya blooms in pinky orange.

'Apricot Gem'. Athough not dramatic in flower, this vireya is valued for its hardiness and bushy vigour. It has rounded growth habit, attractive new leaf growth, and trusses of pretty apricot flowers.

'Aravir'. Similar to 'Felicitas'. The delicious scent of the surprisingly large white trumpet flowers is irresistible. A medium-sized, compact shrub with soft green foliage, it can take some shade.

'Arne Jensen'. A medium-sized bushy shrub, this hybrid had soft green, shiny foliage and excellent full trusses of fragrant blooms.

'Arthur's Choice'. Tough and low-spreading, this small shrub grows well in containers, hanging baskets and garden borders. The flowers are bright orange-red.

'Athanasius'. This hybrid with medium, bushy growth bears trusses of vivid red-orange flared trumpet flowers which are long-lasting.

'Avalon'. A compact plant suited to container culture, 'Avalon' bears spectacular full-domed trusses of pale yellow flowers with wavy edges.

'Bellenden Coral'. A Michael Cullinane (New Zealand) hybrid, this is a vigorous-growing vireya with flowers shaded coral-pink to magenta, and does equally well in containers or in the ground.

'Bernadette'. Highly recommended by Bovees Nursery (USA), 'Bernadette' has slow, compact growth but develops into a superb all-round plant with handsome trusses of bi-toned pink, fluted and ruffled flowers. Deliciously fragrant.

'Blush Tumble'. This miniature, with attractive mid-green leaves and salmon flowers standing upright above the foliage, is so low-growing that it is ideal as a pot plant or as a small basket vireya.

'Blushed Spice'. The strong, upright bush has handsome dark foliage, and the flowers, borne in trusses of 10–15 flowers each, are cream with pink edges.

'Bob's Crowning Glory'. In bloom, this is a real show-stopper. The large trusses of very large flowers in deep rose-pink are lightly scented. Although it may be a little slow to flower, it makes an excellent pot or garden plant and can take some shade.

'Bold Janus'. This tall, very elegant shrub bears apricot flowers tinged with pink, lightly perfumed. The foliage is deep green and it makes an excellent container or in-ground garden plant.

'Bonza'. The new foliage on this compact, upright shrub is a pleasing bronze colour; the bell flowers are deep crimson.

'Brightly'. A Blumhardt (New Zealand) hybrid which lives up to its name. The compact habit and shade-tolerance of this plant, together with its glossy dark foliage and glowing, orange-to-red flowers, make it very desirable. It flowers often, and from a young age.

'Bronze Warrior'. This is a tough and beautiful Australian hybrid with a flower colour like no other. The open trusses of flowers are a rich, coppery orange shade. Its *macgregorei* parentage makes it hardy and reliable when grown in either ground or container, or possibly in a basket.

'Brunei Bay'. A classic plant with unusual needle-like leaves on a twiggy, compact bush, the flowers of 'Brunei Bay' are beautiful clear coral-pink bells. It makes an excellent small container shrub.

'Burgundy Surprise'. The leaves are large and shiny, the bush upright, and the flowers are a sumptuous red-burgundy. Very choice.

'Buttermaid'. Very similar to 'Flamenco Dancer', 'Buttermaid' has slightly more golden, richer yellow flowers in full trusses.

'Buttermilk'. A tall, upright shrub with large furry leaves and trusses of cream trumpets with deeper yellow throats. There are not many vireyas with really good cream flowers but this is one, with the added bonus of scent.

'Cair Paravel'. This hybrid is a sturdy, tall-growing vireya with large shiny leaves and huge ruffled strong pink flowers (10–15 in a truss).

'Calavar'. As yet 'Calavar' is not a common variety but its large flowers in dusty pink shading to apricot, with creamy yellow throats are sure to make it so. It grows into a robust, open bush which is adaptable and free-flowering.

'Cameo Spice'. The perfumed, trumpet flowers on this open-branching bush vary in colour from cream to honey to a quite deep apricot. It's a robust plant with heavily felted leaves. 'Pindi Pearl' is very similar.

'Cape Cod Cranberry'. This bushy, robust shrub bears scented flowers to match the name: deep pink-red.

'Cape Cod Sunshine'. The flowers of this upright, strong-growing vireya vary from light, greenish yellow to light orange-yellow and strong orange.

'Carillon Bells'. This is one of the very best miniature vireyas. Its compact habit and almost perpetual flowering make it ideally suited to tub culture and to hanging baskets if trained. The leaves are glossy and the surprisingly large flowers are salmon-pink.

'Cecilia'. This handsome hybrid has large, very dark leaves, moderate to tall upright growth, and bears luminous dark red buds which unfold into huge white flowers. An added attribute is the rich fragrance.

'Charming Valentino'. As yet not widely known, this is a superb all-round plant because its bushy, medium-growth habit lends itself to growing in containers, in the ground, in hanging baskets, and in particular to growing in standard form. The flowers are a deep pink-red.

'Cherry Liqueur'. Deliciously scented and quick to flower, this one is well named. Its upright habit and bold foliage make it well suited to garden landscaping, where its seductive cherry-red and cream flowers make an arresting sight. It needs judicious pruning, especially when young.

'Cherry Pie'. A Mark Jury (New Zealand) hybrid, this one has a spreading, bushy habit which makes it an excellent container plant. It has glossy foliage and trusses of cherry pink flowers, freely blooming. Very showy.

'Chimbu Glow'. A Blumhardt (New Zealand) hybrid, 'Chimbu Glow' bears vivid red-orange flower trusses which stand above the foliage. It's one of the few narrow, upright vireyas, which could have advantages when positioned in the garden, especially as it appears to be particularly cold-tolerant.

'Coral Flare'. An ideal garden, tub, or basket plant because of its low spreading habit, 'Coral Flare' bears long-lasting coral-pink flowers. It's an excellent performer: a recommended beginner's vireya.

'Cordial Orange'. If it didn't flower this would still be an attractive shrub, for the narrow leaves are glossy and the bush has a slender, upright habit. The flowers bloom in small trusses of intense, burnished orange. It does best in part shade.

'Craig Faragher'. A little miniature that is almost always in flower, this is a treasure of a plant. It's ideal for hanging baskets where it displays to perfection the dainty flowers in varying shades of pink.

'Cream Delight'. A Blumhardt (New Zealand) hybrid, this sturdy, strong-growing shrub has tubular, scented flowers in showy trusses. They're a soft, honey-cream shade with ruffled edges.

'Cressy'. A tidy upright plant well suited to small gardens or containers, 'Cressy' has glossy foliage and long, curved, tubular flowers in luscious cream and pink. Lightly scented.

'Christopher John'. A medium to large bush with strong, open growth, its very large, scented flowers are vibrant pink with cream fading to white throats. Fast flowering, and eye-catching.

'Cyprian'. A vireya of exceptionally striking foliage which turns a shining coppery colour in the sun, 'Cyprian' bears maize-yellow to orange flowers. The long-lasting flowers and handsome foliage, together with robust growth, make it well suited to both garden culture and to large containers.

'Cyril'. The long-lasting flowers of pale, satiny yellow, edged with pale pink and richly scented make 'Cyril' a prized hybrid. The plant is sturdy and tall but slow-growing.

'Dawn Chorus'. This well known Blumhardt (New Zealand) hybrid has glossy leaves and upright, bushy habit; and it reliably produces trusses of medium-sized flowers in pastel pink and cream. It's a good container plant.

'Devil's Delight'. A small, upright shrub with compact, bushy foliage, this little cultivar covers itself with brilliant red flowers when in bloom. As a standard, it's a rare find.

'Dr Herman Sleumer'. A sturdy bush with large, felted leaves and similar in appearance to 'Silken Shimmer', this hybrid, appropriately named in recognition of the vireya pioneer, bears satiny pink trumpets, large and scented, which have creamy yellow throats. This vireya is a natural hybrid.

'Dr Herman Sleumer' x *leucogigas*. The seedlings from this cross are all magnificent. They display huge leaves and enormous waxy flowers in various colours of the white, soft pink, and strong pink range. They flower profusely and are richly scented. Some named forms of this cross include 'Rio Rita' (registered), 'Big Softy' and 'Rangitoto Rose'.

'Doris Mossman'. This small twiggy shrub has thin, dark green leaves that are needle-like and a lot like its parent, the species *stenophyllum*, but a lot easier to grow. The flowers are shiny, red-orange, waxy bells. It's very suited to small container or hanging basket cultivation.

'Dresden Doll'. With lime-green leaves often edged with red, this need not be in flower to command attention. It is not as tough as some hybrids, but when in flower the superb trusses of apricot-pink-cream flowers make a choice display. The compact, upright vireya performs best in moderate shade.

'Elegant Bouquet'. With upright, bushy growth, this hybrid produces big, creamy white flowers that are pleasantly scented. As good-quality white and cream vireyas are not as numerous as other colours, 'Elegant Bouquet' is a prized hybrid.

'Elizabeth Ann Seton'. An easy, bushy shrub with dark green leaves, and reddish buds, veins and midrib, this hybrid bears superb rounded trusses of soft pink, flared, tubular flowers. It's an ideal container plant.

'Esprit de Joie'. Tall, bushy and growing to about 2 m tall, 'Esprit' bears large flowers of gentle rose-pink with cream throats that are pleasingly perfumed.

'Fireball'. An excellent Australian hybrid, 'Fireball' is normally spreading in habit and makes a good trailing and basket plant. The foliage is glossy and the flowers are eye-catching vibrant red to match its name.

'Fireplum'. Healthy, shiny foliage, agreeable bushy form and frequency of flowering make 'Fireplum' a deservedly popular hybrid. The bright, cherry-plum flowers have a slightly paler throat.

'First Light'. Clusters of clear, soft pink flowers that bloom repeatedly throughout the year make this an excellent tub and container plant for pastel gardens. The flowers are lightly scented.

'Flamenco Dancer'. A Mark Jury (New Zealand) hybrid, this one is very similar to 'Buttermaid'. It has vigorous upright form and spectacular trusses of pale yellow to gold flowers, often lightly suffused with apricot. As a tall bush for growing in-ground in the garden, it can be effectively underplanted with smaller, lower-growing vireyas.

'Flamingo Bay'. With its rich fragrance and compact habit, this good performer displays peach-gold tube and peach-pink ruffled flowers in a lovely pastel mix of colours.

'Gardenia Odyssey' (syn. 'Gardenia'). This rare beauty is tall and robust with heavily felted leaves and spectacular trusses composed of up to 28 white or creamy white flowers. Sometimes the flowers are suffused with pale pink, and the scent is gorgeous! It's an outstanding hybrid but may require a little more care. (Be patient if you want it.)

'George Budgen'. An exceptionally free-flowering hybrid, the lively 'hot' flower colours of 'George Budgen' are very similar to those of 'Tropic Glow' and 'Simbu Sunset'. The bush shape, though similar, has a neater and slightly more compact habit.

'Gilded Sunrise'. An extremely free-flowering hybrid with crisp yellow flowers often tinged with a halo of orange, this vigorous, upright bush makes a reliable beginner's vireya. It's a highlight in any garden.

'Golden Casket'. This neatly formed plant produces full trusses of soft, pastel yellow flowers nestling in thick foliage. It's a good container plant.

'Golden Charm'. A Jury (New Zealand) cultivar, 'Golden Charm' has coppery foliage set against attractive dark stems and flowers in shades of yellow to apricot. Because it's notably easy to grow — and is hardier than most other vireyas — this is another recommended beginner's plant.

'Goldilocks'. Of unknown ancestry and similar to a *macgregoriae* species, this hardy and adaptable bush bears appealing golden yellow trusses.

'Gossamer Pink'. Similar to 'Candy', 'Lullaby', and 'Greer's White', this medium, compact bush produces delicate trusses of thin, tubular, pink flowers. It makes a very good standard.

'Gossamer White'. With the same form as 'Gossamer Pink', the scented flowers are a shimmering white.

'Great Scent-sation'. An exciting release for a garden site, or for a large container, this strong, spreading shrub bears carmine-pink bells, which, as the name indicates, are large and fragrant.

'Gwenevere'. With attractive, rounded leaves growing on a compact bush, 'Gwenevere' has waxy, white trumpet flowers forming a full coronet shape. The flowers are also sweetly perfumed.

Halo hybrids: Introduced by Duncan and Davies (New Zealand), these are strong, upright growers with large flowers, mostly in bi-coloured combinations of rich pink, orange, salmons and apricots. All have foliage that is large and bold. Named varieties include 'Halo', 'Chiffon Halo', 'Candy', 'Coral Halo', 'Red Picotee', 'Salmon' and 'Sensation'.

'Haloed Gold'. An excellent Blumhardt (New Zealand) hybrid whose assets have been underrated, 'Haloed Gold' is a strong, upright shrub with unusual and striking flowers: from buds they emerge almost green and then turn yellow, with a band of bright orange-red. The petals have an attractive rippled edge. Sun-tolerant.

'Hansa Bay'. With tall, strong growth that branches well, this cultivar bears pastel bi-coloured flowers in pinkish orange recurved petals, fading into a solid gold colour.

'Happy Wanderer'. A low, spreading shrub, this one is ideal for baskets and bears attractive red-orange blooms.

'Hari's Choice'. This is a giant. It grows into a huge, upright bush with foliage that is equally impressive. The similarly large trusses display vivid, crimson flowers.

'Harry Wu'. From a big dark red bud unfolds a truss of 4–5 large, slightly scented flowers the colour of a ripe peach. The tube is deeper reddish gold with dark red pedicel. It's a sturdy shrub and the large heavy leaves grow thickly. (Harry Wu is a courageous Chinese dissident currently under US protection.)

'Highland Arabesque'. The medium-sized and often

low-growing bush has pale, rounded leaves and bears surprisingly large fluted flowers in silvery pink.

'Honey Star'. Very similar to 'Saffron Star' and 'Maid Marion', these are all Blumhardt (New Zealand) hybrids, with honey-apricot flowers. While the flowers of 'Honey Star' are a lighter colour, the other two tend towards a stronger apricot shade.

'Hot Gossip'. A Jury (New Zealand) hybrid, this compact shrub has handsome foliage and trusses of tubular flowers which open light pink and deepen as they age to a rich claret-red. Extra cultivation care may be needed.

'Hot Tropic'. A Blumhardt (New Zealand) hybrid, this narrow, upright bush bears vivid, orange-red flowers with yellow throats.

'Hugh Redgrove'. Admired for its shiny foliage which is bronze-green often darkening to red, this cultivar is low-growing and bears showy flowers in brilliant Orient red. It can be a little tricky to grow but well worth the try.

'Humboldt Bay'. This one has bold, bluish green leaves and strongly branching growth. The highly fragrant flowers, 10–20 to a truss, open from dark red buds into rich coral-pink.

'Iced Primrose'. With upright open growth, this elegant hybrid bears showy trusses of creamy primrose flowers with a hint of pale green in the throat, and highly scented. Pruning is needed.

'Irian Jaya'. With deep green glossy foliage that is often tinged with purple, 'Irian Jaya' has a low, spreading growth habit and bears good trusses of rich pink.

'Ivory Coast'. An exciting Australian hybrid, 'Ivory Coast' has distinctive and unusual flower trusses that are often multiheaded and sometimes double, with the individual flowers being flat-faced and round in an appealing shade of soft ivory-pink. Its upright bush form makes a superb standard.

'Java Light'. Tried and trusted, this very reliable vireya has proved more sun- and heat-resistant than most. It grows into a large shrub with luminous orange or orange-red flowers.

'Java Rose'. With unusual rosebud double florets and short, rounded petal tips of deep orange broadly margined in red, this new Duncan and Davies (New Zealand) hybrid commands attention. The neatly posed flower truss is lightly scented and the bush is sturdy and upright.

'Jean Baptiste'. Quick to flower, this superb recent introduction produces large, ravishingly scented, creamy white flowers, frequently with petaloids making a full centre. Its bushy, upright habit means it will grow well in the garden, or in a large container.

'Jock's Cairn'. This vigorous, handsome plant makes an excellent subject for a large container. It bears very ornamental trusses of tubular-funnel-shaped flowers in pinkish red with deep pink throats.

'John Henry'. With massive leaves, bold and yet fairly compact form, 'John Henry' produces huge flowers in dome-shaped trusses of soft pink — and perfume to stop you in your tracks.

'Just Peachy'. This beauty is an all-round performer. The full trusses of satiny apricot flowers have an appealing shape and the foliage is just as lovely. The almost prostrate form of 'Just Peachy' makes it an outstanding basket and container subject. Indeed, it's one of the most admired of all vireya hybrids as it is almost never without flower.

'Kisses'. A Blumhardt (New Zealand) hybrid and one of his best, this bushy, upright shrub bears magnificent heads of lolly-pink and cream. It's vigorous and grows as well in the ground as in containers. It flowers regularly.

'Kurt Herbert Adler'. This cultivar has medium spreading growth and handsome round leaves in deep green. The flowers are deep rose-pink.

'Larissa'. An easily grown, medium dense bush with light green foliage, 'Larissa' has tubular flowers with wide-spreading petals. They're a soft pink shade with contrasting dark anthers.

'Lemon Light'. Another Blumhardt (New Zealand) hybrid, 'Lemon Light' lives up to its name with scented flowers in a delicate and delicious shade of soft lemon. It has attractive red stems and good foliage on a compact form, growing well in containers.

'Lemon Lovely'. Glossy foliage, open habit and lemon flowers (sometimes lemon-gold) make this an appealing vireya which benefits from pruning when young. Medium-upright habit.

'Leonore Frances'. An American hybrid, this narrow upright vireya features full trusses of cherry-red, lobed flowers with contrasting green-yellow throats. It should be pruned when young.

'Liberty Bar'. An early hybrid, 'Liberty Bar' is strong-growing, semi-upright and adaptable. It bears large, open trusses of eye-catching salmon-rose flowers, blooming repeatedly throughout the year.

'Little Bo Peep'. Another miniature suited to smaller containers and which also makes a superb, small standard, 'Little Bo Peep' is astonishingly floriferous. Year round it bears its white bell flowers with throats blushed pink-red.

'Little Kisses'. Like 'Kisses', this is a Blumhardt (New Zealand) hybrid which needs to be pruned heavily when young, after which it makes an ideal small container plant. The flowers are similar to the bigger version: flared, blush-pink fading to cream at the throat.

'Little Pinkie'. The compact shape and pleasing glossy foliage make this a useful, multi-purpose plant. It grows well when planted out in the garden, it's a good container plant, and it can be trained into a standard. Added to which the flowers, massed and dainty like the name, are perfumed.

'Littlest Angel'. An always popular miniature with low, spreading habit and handsome foliage, this little shrub makes a perfect container or basket plant. The bright red bell flowers are lively and decorative.

'Lochmin'. This is a superb hanging basket plant which seems to have been overlooked by garden centres. Low, wide and compact, its tubular, two-toned pink flowers hang decoratively from bushy foliage.

'Magic Flute'. A well-named hybrid. In flower, this bushy shrub with appealing round leaves smothers itself in large white flowers that are long, tubular and fluted. They're also scented. It's an ideal shrub for tubs, hanging baskets and garden planting.

'Maid Marion'. Similar to 'Honey Star' and 'Saffron Star', this gentle maid produces chiffon flowers with a barely discernible line running through the centre of each petal. Glossy foliage and seductive pale peach flowers on an upright, bushy form make this a choice cultivar.

'Marshall Pierce Madison'. Once seen in flower this hybrid is, by all accounts, unforgettable. The shrub has tall, strong growth, huge leaves and bears massive trusses of rippled, rich pink flowers. And they're fragrant, too. Very rare.

'Milne Bay'. A compact container plant, 'Milne Bay' has small leaves and covers itself with small, pink trumpet flowers hanging in clusters.

'Moonwood'. Perfumed, crystalline-ivory flowers give this a delicate beauty. The fleshy are dark with a velvety surface. It has a compact, spreading habit making it well suited to containers and hanging baskets.

'Mount Pirie'. Because of the tall rangy habit of this hybrid it needs hard pruning when young to encourage bushier growth of the glossy dark green foliage. It bears brilliant deep orange trumpets with dark red stamens, pistil and stigma.

'Nancy Miller Adler'. The bushy shrub is low-growing and has dense, glossy foliage, which, together with the soft pink flowers, make it perfect for growing in containers.

'Ne Plus Ultra'. The Veitch hybrid has always been in demand because of its extra-full clusters of vivid red flowers and waxy leaves. The flowers are long-lasting. It grows and flowers well in containers and would make an excellent standard shrub. Brilliant when in full flower.

'Niugini Firebird'. Similar to 'Java Light', but with flowers that are slightly larger and fuller with a touch more red in the intense colour, this robust hybrid is recommended for its sun-tolerance.

'Oriana'. This vigorous, bushy shrub bears large trusses of small to medium flowers in sunny hues of gold and yellow.

'Pacific Shower'. Prostrate when young, this charming and adaptable vireya usually gains height as it ages. Its spreading habit make it ideal for hanging baskets. The flowers are an exquisite mix of salmon and cream shades.

'Pacific Sundown'. This vireya from Australia is almost always in flower. The medium-size bush produces non-stop flowers in sumptuous tangerine-orange, fading to a paler shade at the throat.

'Paka Cave'. Richly glowing golden yellow flowers with large flaring trumpets are borne on a sturdy plant with large dark green leaves.

'Pastenello'. This can be a little slow to flower but when it does, the full trusses of large pastel yellow flowers are very rewarding — especially for their fragrance. It has big, felted leaves and is suited to garden situations.

'Peach Dream'. The growth habit of this rare and very choice Australian import is lush; but the flowers are more magnificent still. They're peach coloured, well formed, large and fragrant. Outstanding.

'Pendance'. It's a pity that 'Pendance' suffers from frequent mistaken identity, as many hybrids so named are in fact not 'Pendance'. The true version is an upright, medium-sized shrub bearing huge clusters of satiny pink flowers. It requires pruning, particularly when young.

'Pennywhistle'. An unusual, upright miniature, this flowers almost continuously. The elegant shiny leaves and the attractive orange shade of the flowers add to its worth as a plant for small containers.

'Petra'. This shrub has a neat, compact growth habit with small, rounded leaves. The tubular flowers are very pale pink to white, and have bright pink recurved petals and red-tipped stamens. With training it makes a superb container or basket plant.

'Pindi Pearl'. Very similar to 'Cameo Spice'.

'Pink Delight'. A splendid, tried-and-true vireya which is almost always in flower, this has compact, bushy form and bears handsome trusses of rich pink flowers. It's a good beginners' plant.

'Pink Ray'. A very large and robust plant that will grow anywhere, this one is now established as a popular favourite. The soft pink flowers, which are good for picking, are produced in impressive trusses. Outstanding.

'Pink Seedling'. With flowers similar to 'First Light' only richer in colour, this is a lovely garden plant whose compact form and quality flowers always arouse comment. It grows well in containers.

'Popcorn'. Often described as the best commercial white, this upright vireya smothers itself in showy trusses of white flowers with contrasting brown stamens at regular interval throughout the year. It can be made into an appealing standard and performs well in semi-shade.

'Pretty Cotton Candy' . The name may seem a bit precious, but the flowering ability of this semi-prostrate shrub is absolutely outstanding. In fact, it flowers so much it never seems to grow, but that has advantages for container and basket culture. The flowers are pink and white. Give it some shade.

'Queen of Hearts'. A vigorous, upright shrub, this regal hybrid bears soft salmon bell flowers. Reliable.

'Ra'. The flowers of this siren are vibrant red-orange and gold-yellow. Its medium, bushy growth requires some pruning when young, after which it is extremely free-flowering. It's suited to both garden and container growth. 'Ra' is a Blumhardt (New Zealand) hybrid.

'Raspberry Truffle'. A Snell (Australian) hybrid, the bush is medium sized, the foliage is attractive, and the salver-shaped flowers are in a strong raspberry shade and lightly scented.

'Red Adair'. This spectacular new hybrid from Duncan and Davies (New Zealand) produces large trusses of 8–10 trumpet flowers perfectly displayed. They're orange-scarlet, deepening to a rich dark crimson, especially in cooler weather. Bushy habit.

'Red Rooster'. As the name implies, this compact, low-growing shrub with glossy leaves has lively, fire engine red flowers.

'Red Rover'. A repeat flower in deep coral-pink, the special attribute of 'Red Rover' is its ground-covering form that can be used to effect in the garden, and of course in tubs and baskets.

'Red Sox'. This vigorous bush with glossy foliage bears large trumpet blooms in vibrant orange-scarlet deepening to dark scarlet.

'Rob's Favourite'. An old and reliable hybrid that is tolerant of most conditions. This fast-growing, compact vireya produces salmon-pink flower clusters. Easy.

'Rosie Posie'. The flowers are most unusual. They're semi-double, balsam-like, in a light tangerine shade with lemon centres. A bushy plant, it's ideal for containers.

'Saffron Star'. The upright, medium-sized shrub produces elegant trusses of tubular flowers in a soft saffron shade. See 'Honey Star' and 'Maid Marion'.

'St Valentine'. This is a delightful dwarf well suited to pots and hanging baskets. From the ends of the stems dangle scarlet-red bells that are offset by the small waxy leaves.

'San Gabriel'. Pale yellow flowers flecked with pink adorn a well-shaped compact plant with spreading habits. It has basket potential.

'Santa Lucia'. This hybrid bears large pink trusses of light pink flowers with darker centres.

'Satan's Gift'. A Jury (New Zealand) hybrid, this is considered by Mark's wife Abbie to be the best of all their creations. Adaptable, strong-growing, and free-flowering, its yellow blending to orange-red flowers are large and scented.

'Saxon Glow' and 'Saxon Blush'. The salmon flowers of these two compact and well-foliaged vireyas grow in an unusual manner, standing freely above the leaves on long stems. The two are virtually identical except that the colour of 'Saxon Glow's' flowers is slightly brighter.

'Scotchburn White'. In many ways similar to the species *macgregoriae*, 'Scotchburn White' was collected from the wild and is probably a hybrid which occurred naturally. It bears scented clusters of white flowers and has a strong, bushy habit.

'Shantung Rose'. This is a tall, open and upright vireya with lovely leaves in deep green. The flowers, rose-pink with gold throats, are perfumed.

'Shaya'. A Snell (Australian) hybrid (and named in memory of hybridist Graham Snell's pet dog) 'Shaya' grows into a strong, upright bush with rose flowers that have a hint of blue.

'Shepherd's Warning'. Like an orange-red sunrise, the vibrant orange-scarlet trumpet flowers on rounded trusses of this Duncan and Davies (New Zealand) cultivar make an instant display. The flowers are scented, the trusses are full and rounded, and the foliage is rich green.

'Show Stopper'. For a really red flower, look no further than this. As its name implies, the colour is dazzling. It's a medium-sized, bushy shrub with shiny leaves.

'Silken Shimmer'. Very similar to 'Dr Sleumer'.

'Silver Star'. On this upright, bushy vireya the trusses of long, thin, white flowers are tubular and freely borne.

'Silver Thimbles'. A Blumhardt (New Zealand) hybrid, and similar to 'Little Bo Peep', this is a miniature with reddish stems and silvery bell flowers growing from a bush that has a slightly more open habit.

'Simbu Sunset'. Very similar to 'Tropic Glow', this popular plant has large funnel-shaped blooms in a bright tropical orange-yellow. It flowers and flowers.

'Sir George Holford'. This medium, bushy shrub with attractive leaves bears trusses of clear, burnt-orange flowers.

'Souvenir de J. H. Mangles'. A Veitch hybrid, this reliable, medium-sized vireya produces regular trusses of strong, pinky orange flowers.

'Stanton's Glory'. Sun-tolerant, and therefore a good plant for the open garden, 'Stanton's Glory' has strong glossy leaves with bushy, rounded form, and brilliant, clear orange flowers.

'Star Posy'. A remarkably constant flowerer, 'Star Posy' smothers itself in pink, lightly scented flowers.

'Strawberry Parfait'. The very decorative, scented flowers of this hybrid live up to its name: they're a luscious strawberry shade with cream throats, and the petal edges are frilled. The bush is vigorous and well-foliaged.

'Sunny Splendour'. Introduced by Duncan and Davies (New Zealand), 'Sunny Splendour' has long been regarded as one of the best-ever yellows. It's a tidy, small-to-medium shrub which produces soft yellow fluted flowers in large quantities and with rewarding regularity.

'Sunset Fantasy'. The name says it all: here is an intensity of colour and brilliance to quicken the pulse. The flowers — in bright scarlet — are slashed through the centre of each petal with glowing gold. The bushy foliage is enhanced by stems in a strong burgundy shade, the same colour as the new flower bud. Added to these attributes is an upright bushy form and an ability to flower when young.

'Sweet Amanda'. On a strong and upright bush, 'Sweet Amanda' produces flowers which are satiny pink and white, and lightly fragrant. Prune when young.

'Sweet Wendy'. Found in many gardens, 'Sweet Wendy' is deservedly popular, for it flowers so much and so often. Perhaps that's why it's a slow grower. Open and upright, it grows well in the garden and in containers, and reaches about 1 m. The scented flowers are pastel cream and pink.

'Tashbaan'. Unusual in both foliage and flower, this upright vireya, with its long narrow leaves and unique butterscotch flowers, requires early pruning.

'Taylori'. Having been bred well over 100 years ago, 'Taylori' has stood the test of time. It has attractive foliage on vigorous, yet moderate, bushy growth. The flowers are bright pink with pale centres borne in well-shaped trusses.

'Tropic Glow'. Very similar to 'Simbu Sunset', this has slightly smaller flowers. Adaptable and easy, it has been around for a long time and is still regarded as one of the best hybrids.

'Tropic Tango'. A small upright shrub, this excellent hybrid has dark glossy foliage and pretty tubular flowers of soft creamy apricot blending to rich apricot. It does well in tubs and is very free-flowering.

'Vladimir Bukovsky'. Low-growing, adaptable, and with flawless foliage, this is the only spreading basket-type vireya to produce pure orange flowers. They emblazon the bush with their rich, deep orange fading to paler orange throats. As well as basket and container culture, it can be used as a ground-hugging garden plant. Stunning.

'Wattlebird'. Very similar to 'Gilded Sunrise', with more flowers in a truss and a purer yellow colour.

Species for the collector

In some instances several different forms of the same species have been introduced into cultivation.

R. aequabile. Sumatra. A compact plant with foliage thickly covered with reddish brown scales that easily distinguish it from other species. The bell-shaped flowers are orange to brick-red.

R. aurigeranum. Papua New Guinea. The open, tall-growing bush bears full trusses of golden yellow flowers, making it much used as a hybrid parent. The flowers can be spectacular.

R. blackii. Papua New Guinea. The leaves of this species are circular and almost scaleless — unique. It has an upright habit and bears open trusses of bright red tubular flowers.

R. bryophilum. Irian Jaya. This compact plant with small, pale salmon flowers is a reliable bloomer and easy to grow. The small leaves and branches are covered with brown scales, which make it distinctive.

R. calignis. Papua New Guinea. A small willowy, fine-leaved shrub, this species has striking golden brown scales and the small hanging flowers are curved and cream-coloured.

R. carringtoniae. Papua New Guinea. Often slow to flower, this medium upright species has bushy foliage and long, thinly curved, tubular flowers which are white and fragrant.

R. christianae. Papua New Guinea. A compact shrub of moderate growth with a tendency to be willowy, this has small yellow-orange flowers and has been used for many hybrids.

R. christii. Papua New Guinea. This unusual shrub with leaves appearing in whorls on short stems is small and upright. The curved, tubular flowers are a blend of red, yellow and lime-green. There are several forms.

R. commonae. Papua New Guinea. The oval leaves are thick, while the curved, tubular bells which hang from the branch tips of this small, upright shrub vary in colour. There are cream, pink and deep red forms.

R. crassifolium. Northern Borneo, Sabah and Sarawak. *Crassifolium* is very variable. The large leaves are usually thick and leathery with prominent veining. The flower colour is often red-orange, but varies, and appears also as pink, pink-orange and even white.

R. cruttwellii. Papua New Guinea. A well-branched shrub of moderate to tall height, this has large obovate leaves and fragrant flowers that are slender, tubular and pure white. (Named after Norman Cruttwell, the British missionary who searched for and identified many Papua New Guinea species.)

R. fallacinum. Northern Sabah. This species has brown furry foliage, especially when young, which turns silver with age. A tall shrub, it bears full trusses of strong, red-orange flowers. It is different — and difficult to cultivate.

R. goodenoughii. Papua New Guinea. An exceptionally attractive, white-flowering species, this bears shiny leaves and upward-curving tubular flowers which are beautifully scented.

R. gracilentum. Papua New Guinea. A small, compact,

90

spreading bush with shiny wedge-shaped leaves. The fine stems and neat miniature flowers in rose-pink or red shades are tubular, and grouped in twos and threes. This species prefers cool roots.

R. helwigii. Papua New Guinea. A real collector's plant, *helwigii* is outstanding. The thick leaves are furry and rounded; the bush is strong and upright; the buds are unique in the way they develop from a bud whorl and seem to take forever to open, and the curved, tubular flowers are sizzling red.

R. herzogii. Papua New Guinea. Noted for its fragrant white flowers borne in trusses of flared tubes and for its attractive grey-green leaves, this species has an upright form and moderate growth habit.

R. himantodes. Borneo. A rare, needle-leafed species, this is often seen in the wild in unexpectedly shady areas. The twiggy shrub bears rounded, white flowers which strikingly contrast with prominent brown anthers; and highly decorative spotting on the backs of the flowers.

R. jasminiflorum var. *punctatum*. Malay Peninsula and Sumatra. A commonly grown species because of its scented clusters of long tubular pink flowers and its adaptability to baskets and containers, its bushy, sprawling shape make it a good species for small gardens.

R. javanicum. Islands of the South Pacific. An extremely variable species, this upright bush has bold, glossy foliage which requires pruning when young. Because it is native to many different areas the flower colour varies according to location, from yellow to bright orange. In cultivation for one hundred years, *javanicum* is easy to grow and to flower.

R. konorii. Papua New Guinea. *Konorii* is popularly grown for its very large and highly scented white or soft pink trumpets. The leaves are thick and furry and the growth habit is medium bushy. It can be slow-growing.

R. laetum. West Irian Jaya. A sun-tolerant species with delectable, clear, luminous yellow flowers, *laetum* tends to grow into a tall and straggly bush if not pruned when young.

R. lochae. Australia. A species native to the far north of Queensland, *lochae* is always compact and bushy. The flowers, which are long-lasting, are usually bell-shaped and deep pink to red. There are various forms.

It is the parent of many excellent hybrids.

R. loranthiflorum. Solomon Islands. The light green glossy foliage and thin white tubular flowers on a compact, upright bush make this a good, all-round species for the garden. The flowers are lightly scented.

R. macgregoriae. Papua New Guinea. Many forms of this species have been collected. It has strong, bushy growth habit and bears neat trusses in many shades, usually yellow to orange. Easy and adaptable.

R. orbiculatum. Sabah, Brunei, Sarawak. As the name suggests, the leaves of *orbiculatum* are rounded; they grow on short stems from a compact bush which bears extraordinarily large, long tubular flowers of soft pink. The flowers open out to a flat face and are lightly scented. It is often described as being orchid-like in appearance.

R. pauciflorum. Malay Peninsula. With round bright green leaves on a charming compact plant, this one is well suited to hanging baskets. Small, waxy red flowers bloom singly or in pairs.

R. phaeochitum. Papua New Guinea. Elegant and upright, *phaeochitum* is very free-flowering, especially for a species. The pink flowers are curved and tubular and the new foliage is scaled with a coppery red colour of great appeal.

R. phaeopeplum. Papua New Guinea. Though slow to bloom, the large flowers are pinkish white and fragrant. They grow on a moderate to tall bush which Dr Sleumer described as a smaller version of the species *R. konorii*.

R. pneumonanthum. Borneo. A surprising species with coppery foliage and most unusual flower buds, *pneumonanthum* reveals full trusses of scented, tubular, near-white flowers. It is a small upright shrub.

R. polyanthemum. Borneo. This is a collector's plant. It's a slow grower with distinctive dark brown scales on the leaves and flowers that are rich orange-red and sometimes scented.

R. praetervisum. Borneo, Sabah. A small upright shrub with dangling, thin curved flowers, this species is noteworthy for its flower colour — pink-violet. It is likely to play an important role in producing future hybrids.

R. rarum. Papua New Guinea. Easy to grow and to flower, this unusual small vireya has a compact and almost vine-like shape with narrow pointed leaves on long stems. The rose-red hanging flowers make it a good hanging-basket plant.

R. retivenium. Borneo, Sabah. The leaves are dark and glossy and the growth habit is upright. It needs hard pruning when young. The flowers, which are sometimes scented, are a superb clear yellow.

R. rubineiflorum. Papua New Guinea. A prostrate spreading plant to 10 cm tall, this unusual species has thin wiry stems bearing shiny leaves. The red bell flowers which stand above the foliage for several months in summer are relatively large on a prostrate plant with very small leaves. It's a good subject for a small pot or ponga hollow.

R. rugosum. Borneo, Sabah. This species is common in the wild but tricky in cultivation. The dark green leaves are unusually wrinkled. The flowers are plum-pink.

R. scabridibracteum. Papua New Guinea. This species is exceptional: the appearance of the leaves could be described as metallic — making an intriguing combination with the rich red flowers.

R. sessilifolium. Sumatra. An upright, compact, bushy plant with shiny foliage, this bears full trusses of clear, soft yellow flowers.

R. stenophyllum. Northern Borneo. *Stenophyllum* has the distinction of having remarkably narrow, needle-like leaves, so that it is almost unrecognisably vireyan. In the wild it grows in unexpectedly shady situations. The waxy bell flowers are a strong orange-red and the plant is suited to baskets and small containers.

R. suaveolens. Northern Borneo, Sabah. With rounded, short-stemmed leaves, this species has white flowers with an unusual scent. Descriptions of the scent vary; some say the flowers smell like liquorice. *Suaveolens* is suited to hanging baskets.

R. superbum. Papua New Guinea. Rare, and sometimes difficult to grown in cultivation, this bears flowers to match its name: superb. They're exceptionally large, creamy white and sometimes suffused with pink, and highly scented. The large leaves are heavily indumented when young.

R. tuba. Papua New Guinea. The surprisingly long, tubular flowers (hence the name) of this species are decoratively arranged and flower en masse. They're white or white-blended-pink, and scented, and are offset with dark green leaves on an upright bush.

R. wrightianum. Papua New Guinea. A small, upright shrub with dark foliage, this species has very dark red flowers. *Wrightianum* var. *wrightianum* flowers have the deepest red of any and they can be described as red-black.

R. zoelleri. Papua New Guinea, Moluccas. *Zoelleri* is so adaptable and produces such brilliant flowers that it has been justifiably popular with hybridisers. It's a strong, upright shrub with variable bi-coloured flowers in yellow and orange.

Note: Some species collected in the wild are so extremely variable that sometimes their identity is suspect. For plant hunters the difficulties lie in establishing the identity of a plant not in flower; in being certain that a species is in fact a true species and not a natural hybrid — of which there are many; and when collecting seed, in trying to ensure that the seed is pure. Even experts disagree. Botanists in Australia, for example, have long believed that only one species (*lochae*) was endemic, and that all variations were but forms of this single species, but recently they agreed that one form was in fact a new species. Taxonomical clarity remains elusive.

Index

Conversion charts

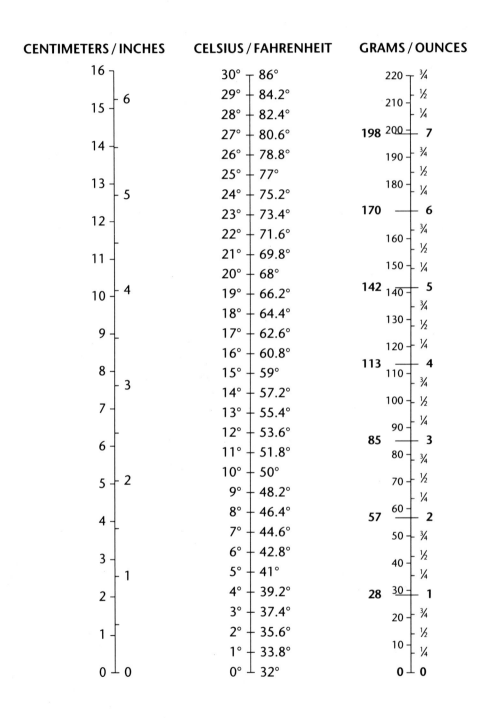

CENTIMETERS / INCHES

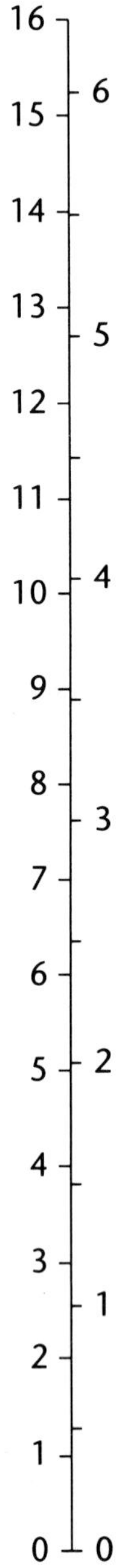
16
15
14
13
12
11
10
9
8
7
6
5
4
3
2
1
0
6
5
4
3
2
1
0

CELSIUS / FAHRENHEIT

Celsius	Fahrenheit
30°	86°
29°	84.2°
28°	82.4°
27°	80.6°
26°	78.8°
25°	77°
24°	75.2°
23°	73.4°
22°	71.6°
21°	69.8°
20°	68°
19°	66.2°
18°	64.4°
17°	62.6°
16°	60.8°
15°	59°
14°	57.2°
13°	55.4°
12°	53.6°
11°	51.8°
10°	50°
9°	48.2°
8°	46.4°
7°	44.6°
6°	42.8°
5°	41°
4°	39.2°
3°	37.4°
2°	35.6°
1°	33.8°
0°	32°

GRAMS / OUNCES

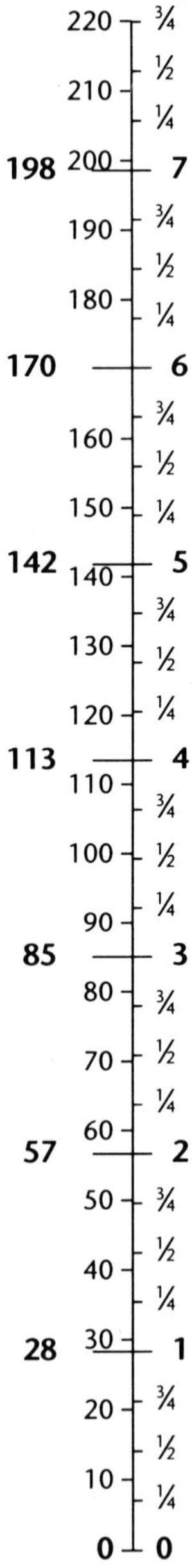
220 ¾
½
210
¼
198 200 7
¾
190
½
180
¼
170 6
¾
160
½
150 ¼
142 140 5
¾
130
½
120 ¼
113 110 4
¾
100 ½
¼
90
85 3
80 ¾
70 ½
¼
60
57 2
50 ¾
½
40
¼
28 30 1
20 ¾
½
10 ¼
0 0